The Truth About RV Living

The Good, the Bad, and the Ugly

By Jerry Minchey

www.LifeRV.com

Stony River Media

ISBN-13: 978-1-947020-12-2

1. Recreational vehicle living.

Published by Stony River Media

Knoxville, Tennessee

StonyRiverMedia.com

Disclaimer

The information in this book is based on the author's knowledge, experience and opinions. The methods described in this book are not intended to be a definitive set of instructions. You may discover other methods and materials to accomplish the same end result. Your results may differ.

There are no representations or warranties, express or implied, about the completeness, accuracy or reliability of the information, products, services, or related materials contained in this book. The information is provided "as is," to be used at your own risk.

This book is not intended to give legal or financial advice and is sold with the understanding that the author is not engaged in rendering legal, accounting or other professional services or advice. If legal or financial advice or other expert assistance is required, the services of a competent professional should be sought to ensure you fully understand your obligations and risks.

This book includes information regarding the products and services of third parties. I do not assume responsibility for any third-party materials or opinions. Use of mentioned third-party materials does not guarantee your results will mirror those mentioned in the book.

All trademarks appearing in this book are the property of their respective owners.

Version 2019.03

Dedicated to my parents, Charles and Helen Minchey, who taught me to embrace traveling and enjoy life.

Table of Contents

Introduction 1

Chapter 1: No One Tells You the Whole Story about RVing ... 9

Chapter 2: Is This What I Signed up for?............................. 23

Chapter 3: You're Worrying about the Wrong Things 35

Chapter 4: Why Do You Want to Live in an RV?................... 41

Chapter 5: "I Wish I Had Waited Longer before I Started
RVing," Said No One 47

Chapter 6: Simplify and Go... 53

Chapter 7: What about Solo RVing?..................................... 59

Chapter 8: What about a Home Base?.................................. 67

Chapter 9: Getting the Courage to Hit the Road.................. 73

Chapter 10: How Much Does the RVing Lifestyle Cost?....... 79

Chapter 11: Making Money While on the Road..................... 87

Chapter 12: A Lifestyle That's Easy to Get into and
Easy to Leave 97

Chapter 13: How to Buy Your First RV................................ 101

Chapter 14: What Are the Real Downsides to RV Living? .. 113

Chapter 15: The Good and Bad Things about Getting Rid of
All Your Stuff 121

Chapter 16: Is the Bad Part of RVing Really All that Bad?. 129

Chapter 17: You Have to Hit the Road before You're Ready. 133

Chapter 18: Why Haven't You Made a Decision?............... 137

Chapter 19: Summing It All Up... 149

Chapter 20: Other Resources 151

Did You Like This Book? 183

Introduction

"The Lord moves in mysterious ways, but you don't have to. Use your turn signals."

—Anonymous

After you read this book, you might start thinking that RVing books, blogs, and YouTube videos have been lying to you about how wonderful the RVing life is. They're not really lying to you, but, for sure, they're not telling you the whole story.

We would all like to continue believing that RVing is all sunsets, campfires, and margaritas. But the truth is that there are a lot of bad and even ugly parts of living the RV life.

Not enough bad things to make me change my mind about loving this life, but they might change your mind when you realize how bad things can really be.

I've never heard anyone say, "I wish I had waited longer before I started RVing." They all say they wish they had made the decision and started a lot sooner.

If you think you might want to live full time in an RV (and you must be thinking that or you wouldn't have bought this book), then you're on the right path. You're doing your homework, learning about the lifestyle and getting your questions answered.

Some people get stranded in this phase and never feel like they have all the answers. The truth is they don't. You will never know everything you need to know to hit the road. There will always be a lot of unknowns and "What if" questions in your mind. Accept the fact that:

Every decision you make for the rest of your life will be made with incomplete information

Accept that fact. The decision to start living in an RV is no different. Accept this fact and move forward.

Do a reasonable amount of research, get answers to most of your questions, and make your decision, make your plan and then make it happen. I think most people spend more time planning a two-week vacation than they do planning their lives.

Does that describe you? How much time have you spent actually planning what you want to do with your life right now? It's not too late. You can change now; plan what you want to do now. It doesn't have to be how you live the rest of your life.

In Chapter 13 I'll show you how and why the RVing lifestyle is the easiest to get into and the easiest to get out of. You won't be taking a big risk if you start living in an RV.

Fear is the real thing holding you back

No one likes to admit that fear is keeping them from making a decision or taking action, but if you're honest with yourself, you know that fear is the only thing holding you back.

You have a lot to learn before you can make an informed decision about whether RVing is the right life for you.

If you've done much research about RVing by watching YouTube videos, reading books, or following RVing blogs, I'm sure you've heard a lot about how wonderful the lifestyle is.

But there's more to the lifestyle than just the fun part. Most of the bad things about RVing are told as funny stories if they are even told at all.

Will Rogers said, *"Everything is funny if it's happening to somebody else."*

Probably, if you've heard any bad things about the RV lifestyle, you've heard it in the form of a funny story. Even the cover of this book follows that format and shows something bad about RVing, but it's shown in a way to make it seem funny. The reason it's funny is because it's happening to somebody else.

Let's get on with the facts and learn the good, the bad, and the ugly parts of the RV lifestyle.

Finally, there's a book (this one) that tells you the truth about living in an RV

In this book I'll take you on a personal and inspiring journey into the real world of full-time RV living. I'll share the experience and wisdom I've gained from my seven years on the road as a full-time RVer. I'll give you heartfelt advice and share intimate anecdotes that will make you feel like you have shared the experiences with me.

In this book, I don't sugarcoat anything. This book covers the good, the bad, and the really bad parts of the RVing lifestyle.

This book tells it like it is in a way no other book has done before. My previous 10 books about living in an RV have probably made some parts of the lifestyle sound more glamorous, exciting, and fun than they really are. It's easy to get carried away when talking about how wonderful and enjoyable the RVing lifestyle is.

How this book is different from other RVing books

- It's based on my seven years of full-time RV living.

- It debunks the over-hyped glamour of the RV life and digs into what it's really like to live and travel full time in an RV on a day-to-day basis.

- It provides a dynamic new look at the real challenges of living, traveling and working in an RV as a couple, a family, or as a solo RVer.

- In this book you'll find real-life stories of RV life on the road that pack a punch of insight, humor, and emotions.

Telling someone about RVing is like talking about grandkids or pets

Most people tend to talk about all the good and wonderful things and leave out the bad, heartbreaking, and expensive parts. Maybe not intentionally, but it's just human nature to remember and talk about the good times when it comes to RVing, grandkids, and pets.

The RVing lifestyle is not all sunsets, campfires, and margaritas, but enough of it is to make a lot of people decide that they don't want to live any other way.

Of course, not everyone feels this way. It's not the right lifestyle for everyone. Maybe it's not the right lifestyle for you. If it's not the right lifestyle for you, it's better to find that out before you sell everything and hit the road.

That's the purpose of this book. It's not to talk you into living full time in an RV or talk you out of it. The purpose of this book is to arm you with truth and facts that no one else tells you so you can make an informed decision.

By the time you finish reading this book, you will know some wonderful things about the RVing lifestyle that you had not heard about before. But you'll also know some bad things (and some really bad things) that you had not heard about before either.

Having a problem-solving mindset and attitude is a great thing to have as an RVer. Don't worry if that doesn't describe you. It's something you will develop as you continue RVing.

"If you take risks, you're going to be wrong as much as you're right. And that is the pain of life and the joy of life."

—Hollywood Pioneer, Sherry Lansing

Bottom Line: RVing is a wonderful life, but it's probably way different from anything you've ever done or experienced before. It's not for everybody. In addition to the practical changes you'll experience, the emotional aspects of the new lifestyle are way more than many people are prepared to deal with.

I think you'll find that the good parts about the RVing lifestyle are way better than you imagined, but there are bad things about the RVing life that are way worse than you realized or expected.

Don't make your decision about RVing yet. Read the rest of this book and then decide if RVing is right for you.

Chapter 1

No One Tells You the Whole Story about RVing

"Men occasionally stumble over the truth, but most of them pick themselves up and hurry off as if nothing had happened."

—Winston Churchill

I think what old Winston said about the truth describes a lot of us when it comes to hearing things we don't want to hear and for sure it describes most people after they've been bitten by the RVing bug.

Anything they hear bad about living in an RV goes in one ear and out the other.

There are many things about the RVing life that are different from the way you're living now. A lot of these things you know about and are expecting.

After all, if living in an RV was going to be the same as living in a stick-and-brick house, why would you want to make the change?

You're probably familiar with a lot of the things that will be different (maybe even most of them), but in this chapter, I'm going to tell you about some of the most important things to expect that you probably haven't been told about.

Later in the book, I'll tell you some of the myths about RVing. In other words, some of the things you've been told that just ain't true.

Here's one thing to keep in mind while you're reading the rest of this chapter.

"Adventure is allowing the unexpected to happen to you."

—Richard Aldington

Some things people don't tell you about RVing

1. New RVs have a lot of problems.

This is one thing you may not have been told, but even if you were told, you probably took it with a grain of salt. When you buy a new car, one of the main advantages is that you won't likely have any maintenance problems for a few years. The reliability of new cars is amazing.

Just the opposite is true for new RVs. It's hard to believe, but it's true. You can (and should) expect a lot of problems with a new RV. Don't dare buy a new RV and hit the road. Live in your RV for a month or two— even if it's in your driveway.

Also, take some short trips, so you'll get to know your RV, and so you can find out some of the problems that the dealer needs to fix.

Most of the problems will be fixed under warranty but not necessarily in a timely manner.

I have heard of kitchen cabinets falling off the wall, air conditioners not working, water leaks (these are common), and the list goes on and on. You might wonder how new RVs could have so many problems. It's simple. Cars, trucks, and SUVs are built on an assembly line, but RVs are built one at a time.

A crew of about a half a dozen workers does everything on the RV. The same worker does the plumbing, the electrical, the carpentry work, etc.

If someone is working on an assembly line putting a bolt in the same hole all day long, it's hard to get that wrong. But when they're building a complete RV, I think you can see how there could be a lot of things that don't get done exactly right.

The whole goal of RV manufacturers is to build the RV at the lowest cost possible. The plan is to build the RV fast knowing that some things will not be done exactly right and then factor in paying the RV dealer to fix all the things that were not done correctly.

You might think this is not a good business plan, but it has worked for years. The price of an RV would go up considerably if they slowed the building process down, added inspectors, and did everything they could to turn out an RV with no problems. Buyers don't want to pay the price to get a more or less perfect RV.

I guess I can agree with this philosophy, but the part I disagree with is that the dealer doesn't tell the buyer that he is going to find a lot of things wrong with the RV. He does say that if you find anything wrong, bring it back and we will fix it—and they will, but not necessarily in a timely manner.

It is what it is. Accept the fact that a lot of things are going to go wrong with any new RV. That's one of the many reasons I recommend that you don't buy a new RV as your first RV. I'll go into more details on this in Chapter 13 about buying your first RV.

2. Get RV repairs done in the offseason if possible.

If you buy a new RV, it will come with a warranty, but most RVers use their RVs during the summer months, and RV repair centers and mobile techs are sometimes backed up for months during the summer. RV repair shops in Florida, Arizona, and south Texas are busy during the winter snowbird months.

Also, many RV manufacturers pay RV dealers about 60% of their going shop rate to do warranty work. Whether RV dealers tell you this or not, think about it. If you owned an RV repair shop and had a three-month backlog of work to be done, would doing warranty work be very high on your priority list?

If you have any repairs or warranty work that you know you're going to need to have done, try to get the work done in the offseason if possible.

3. The Internet is not available at all camping locations.

And for sure fast, reliable internet is not available at a lot of places. Even if the campground says they have fast, free Wi-Fi, it may be kind of true. They have Wi-Fi. It's good (or at least, okay) on this side of the campground, or near the office, but not good on the other side (where you are). There are Wi-Fi boosters you can buy and having Wi-Fi hot spots with different carriers will help, but if you have to have a fast, reliable Internet for your work, RVing can be a big problem.

Like almost all RVing problems, there are solutions to Wi-Fi problems. To see the latest solutions and equipment reviews to help you get Wi-Fi while RVing, check out Chris and Cherie's RV Mobile Internet website at https://www.rvmobileinternet.com

4. Dumping the black tank

Dumping the black tank is one of the problems people like to talk about when they're talking to other RVers. It's like saying, "You ain't heard nothing yet." But you don't usually hear them talking about it to non-RVers.

By the way, you can't be a snob if you're holding a sewer hose.

Like a lot of problems with the RV life, there are solutions. The typical RV sewer hose will cost you about $15 to $35, but for $119 you can get a much better one. This sewer hose I'm talking about is expensive, but it solved all my black tank dumping problems. It stays connected with a CAM lock connector that ensures a leak-proof connection to the sewer outlet. I never disconnect mine. It also has a handle and a shut-off valve on the other end.

Here's a link to where you can see a picture of it and get it on Amazon. This is not an affiliate link. https://www.amazon.com/dp/B010X65OHE

I have been using this hose for three years and I have never touched a drop of black water in the three years. I've never seen another one of these green sewer hoses in a campground. I don't know if other RVers don't know about them or if they just don't want to spend the money to fix the problem.

While everybody else is sitting around the campfire telling horror stories about dumping their black tank, I just sit back and listen and enjoy the stories.

As Will Rogers said, *"Everything is funny as long as it's happening to somebody else."*

5. You're going to have uninvited guests.

I'm not talking about your mother-in-law and her new boyfriend. I'm talking about mice. I don't care how new or old your RV is, accept the fact that you're going to get mice in your RV. Don't panic (well, go ahead and panic if that helps, but you still have to deal with getting rid of the mice). Your attack plan for dealing with mice should be two-fold.

First, seal every hole you can find. Stop the hole up with steel wool. Mice can and will chew through about anything else. Mice can climb up the power cord, water hose, sewer hose, and they can jump from the ground up to the chassis and if there's a way to get inside your living area or into your storage bins, they will find it. If there's not a way, they'll chew a hole and make a way. It's a constant battle.

The second part of the plan is to get rid of the mice after they get inside your RV. There are traps, poisons, sticky sheets, and you can use smells that mice don't like, such as Irish Spring soap, mothballs, bags of bark that smell like a Christmas tree, and the list goes on and on.

I've tried all of these techniques. They all seem to help somewhat, but the best way I've found to get rid of mice is to use an old-fashioned mousetrap. I keep traps in the storage bins, under the kitchen sink, under the sofa, and anywhere I've seen signs that a mouse has ever been. Of course, I check the traps every few days and change the bait from time to time. If the bait gets old or hard, mice won't eat it. I've had the best luck with cheese and with peanut butter. I sometimes use one and sometimes I use the other.

No one tells you that you're going to have to put up with mice problems, but accept the fact and deal with it. There's no need to get frustrated (and it won't help if you do).

I guess I didn't follow all of these techniques. I put my motorhome in storage and went to Costa Rica for three months. The storage fee was only $30 a month, and I canceled my collision insurance for the three months and that saved me $130 a month, so I came out $100 a month ahead.

The problem was that Mickey, Minnie, and several of the other mice in the neighborhood found out I was gone, so they moved in.

I had a lot of cleaning to do when I got back. The motorhome needed a good deep cleaning anyway, but it wasn't something I was planning on doing as soon as I got back.

I used some mouse traps and got rid of the mice in short order. Now all is well, plus, I have a thoroughly cleaned RV.

I'll probably go back to Costa Rica again for a few months next year, but for sure I will do a better job of stopping up holes, and I'll put out several mouse traps and have someone check them once a week.

Some things are not problems—it's just your attitude

Here are some so-called problems that fit into this category.

- I saw a post on Facebook the other day where a guy said the biggest problem with RVing was not having room for a printer. That's an attitude problem. There is plenty of room in an RV (even in a van) for a small wireless printer. If you really can't find room for a printer (and you want one), get rid of a pair of shoes and you'll have plenty of room for a small printer. I use my printer all the time, and I wouldn't want to be without it.

  Maybe you don't want or need a printer, but don't say there's no room for one in your RV.

- Another so-called problem I hear people talking about is not being able to take a long hot shower. If you're in a bathhouse at a campground, you can take a long hot shower.

  If you're in your RV, you have six gallons (some RVs have 10 gallons) of hot water. That will allow you to take a reasonably long shower. If you want to splurge, you can invest in a continuous hot water system. That way you won't ever run out of hot water.

But if you're boondocking, running out of hot water is not your only concern. You don't want to use up all of your fresh water or fill up your gray water tank. If you start to do that, you will have to take what's called a "navy shower." That means you get wet, turn the water off, lather up, turn the water back on and rinse off.

Complaining about not being able to take a long, hot shower is an attitude problem. You can solve the problem if you want to. It's just a matter of how badly you want to solve the problem.

One way some people solve the problem of how to take a long, hot shower is to join a fitness club like Planet Fitness or one of the other national chains. For $22.95 a month you can have unlimited visits at locations all over the country. We could all use a good workout two or three times a week. It's an option to consider. When you're boondocking, you don't usually take a shower every day anyway. Also, at many truck stops you can take a long, hot shower for $5.

- When it comes to the RVing lifestyle, if a story doesn't concern something fun or interesting to do or it's not a funny story, you probably won't hear about it on YouTube, in a book, in a blog or on Facebook. Occasionally you will see a YouTube video or a blog with the title *The seven worst things about RVing* or some similar title, but not often. These are worth watching or reading, but a lot of times they are just petty things or funny things and not real problems.

- Another thing that RVers complain about is not having a garbage disposal. Don't put table scraps down the kitchen drain. These end up in the gray tank and they don't always flush out completely.

- Not having a dishwasher is something you will have to get used to. Some of the newer, expensive RVs will have a dishwasher, but these are few and far between. I think most people know about not having a dishwasher before they start RVing, so this is usually not a surprise.

- Having a smaller refrigerator than most people are used to is another thing you will have to get used to. You can get the larger, conventional refrigerators in an RV, but they take up more of your valuable space. If there are more than two people in your family, a larger refrigerator might be a worthwhile modification to make to your RV.

- Other than taking up a lot of space, another disadvantage of having a large, conventional refrigerator is that it runs on electricity only. Ordinary RV refrigerators run on electricity or propane, so boondocking where you don't have access to electricity is no problem.

- When two people are in an RV, if one is walking around, the other one will feel the RV shake. You don't notice this if you're the only person in the RV, but with two or more people it can be quite noticeable.

  There's an old RVing joke that says, "If this RV is rocking, don't come knocking." But it could just be rocking because someone is walking around.

- Accept the fact that an RV kitchen is a "one-butt" kitchen. Having someone trying to help you fix a meal usually slows things down more than it helps.

- If you like to watch a lot of TV, you might be in for some disappointment. Some campgrounds have cable, but I've found these services to be flaky. You can crank up the TV antenna on the roof of your RV and pick up a few local broadcast stations. Sometimes this works great, and sometimes it doesn't work at all.

  I have an unlimited Wi-Fi service and I use the Amazon Fire Stick to watch TV.

  If you're really into watching a lot of TV and want to be sure you don't miss a game or your favorite program, you can invest in a satellite system. A lot of RVers do this.

13 Reasons You'll Regret an RV in Retirement

If you really want to know how bad RVing can be, check out this article published by Kiplinger Magazine on Aug. 27, 2019, *13 Reasons You'll Regret an RV in Retirement.* Here's a link to the article.

TinyURL.com/y63znnvt

Just as most books about RVing go overboard making things sound so wonderful, I think this article goes overboard in the opposite direction making the idea of RVing sound very expensive and making it sound like a lifestyle you will regret. After all, that's what the title of the article says.

The article does have some valid points you'll need to consider, but remember that the purpose of the article is to point out how bad retiring and living in an RV will be and it doesn't attempt to point out any good points about the lifestyle or how to buy a used RV and cut the cost way below the numbers they show.

Bottom Line: Accept the fact that you won't know about most of the things you're not going to like until you hit the road and experience them for yourself. Things are going to break, and bad and annoying things, in general, are going to happen.

Go into the RVing adventure with the attitude that crap (literally and figuratively) is going to happen. Adopt the attitude that you can deal with these things, and you might just survive and enjoy the RV lifestyle.

Chapter 2

Is This What I Signed up for?

"The more I learn about people the more I like my dog."

—Mark Twain

One of the best ways to learn what RV living is really like is to talk to people who are actually doing it. Let them tell you about their fears, catastrophes, terrifying moments, and joys. It's all part of the RV lifestyle.

There's no one right way to RV. It depends on your goals, desires, and situation.

Following in this chapter are stories from two RVers who are living the RVing life in totally different ways. They describe some of what they see as the good, bad, and ugly parts of RVing as they have seen and experienced the lifestyle.

RVing Alternatives

My friend Camille Attell and her husband quit their plush corporate jobs and have been living full time in their RV since 2016.

I asked Camille to tell us a little bit about her experiences. Here's her story.

Camille, her husband, Bryce, and their cat, Parker

How RVing Can Transform You (For the Better)

I bet when you think of RVing, you don't think of a life transformation.

You probably picture open roads, sweeping valleys, and grand national parks like Zion in Utah or the Great Smoky Mountains of Tennessee and North Carolina.

The last thing you think of is how transformational RVing can be. But it can be for a lot of people, including me, and that's a good thing.

Merriam-Webster defines transformation as the change in the composition or structure of a thing. Water changes to steam when it boils, caterpillars turn into butterflies— you get the gist.

Now, I've had a few transformational moments in my life—getting a master's degree in counseling after being a terrible student my whole life, summiting Mount Kilimanjaro in Tanzania at 19,341 feet, and getting married stand out.

So how in the world does RVing fit into this category? And how can it transform your life too?

In 2016, my husband Bryce and I walked away from our cushy corporate-America jobs after more than twenty years. We left behind security (or so we thought), our friends, family, and even identities to jump into an RV and see the country. It all sounded so fun and liberating. And it was!

It was also terrifying. That's a lot of change for a person. We pictured all the beauty America had to offer, and while we've seen and continue to see all the magnificence that you're picturing, we weren't exactly prepared for the major life shifts.

So, what is so transformational about RVing? Nothing and everything. It's actually pretty mundane when you break it down. But I'm a deep thinker, and everything means something to me, like the time our bedroom slide broke.

Within a few weeks of hitting the road full-time, our bedroom slide stopped working. It was sticking partially out and wouldn't extend or retract. We were RV newbies and hadn't figured out how to work the systems yet.

I'll make a long story short and tell you that after many phone calls to our manufacturer, lots of Iinternet research, and desperate attempts at pushing and pulling on the slide, we ended up shacking up in a dealer's garage for four days.

This was in Oregon during a nasty rainstorm. There we were in a dealer's garage, with no access to our clothes (because the slide pushed against our drawers), in the rain. It wasn't anything like we had pictured.

As a restless person, I don't much like sitting around with nothing to do. So, I hopped on craigslist and started looking for local jobs. I found four that I could do that weekend! I managed to get hired for two.

I roped my husband into a small acting gig for an educational video about being foster parents. We made $100 for an hour of work. Then we took ourselves to dinner for a celebratory New York strip steak. Life was good. You don't develop that kind of creative problem solving sitting in an office.

I have so many stories like this. Like the time we were so late getting into Dallas, Texas, in the pouring rain (what is it with me and rain?). It was pitch black in the RV park. I stepped out of the coach to guide my husband into the RV space when—BLAMO—I plunged deep into inches of water. It was so cold and wet. My shoes and socks were fully submerged. In fact, because I'm only 5'2" it felt like I was waist-deep in a rushing river.

Cold. Wet. Annoyed.

I looked up angrily into the rain when this feeling of pure joy washed over my body. I started laughing hysterically at how ridiculous it was that I was even annoyed. I mean here I was living my dream. This is what I signed up for!

No, I didn't sign up for broken slides, rainy days or any other inconveniences (which have been a lot). But I did sign up for new experiences and to feel alive again. For too long, I had driven the same route to work, sat at the same desk, and had a very same-y daily experience. I wanted something more interesting and exciting. Be careful what you wish for, right?

Since being on the road Bryce and I have started a blog called MoreThanAWheelin.com, and I launched Remote-Work-School.teachable.com to help people find remote work, Bryce has done financial consulting for RV businesses, we've made wonderful new friends, and we've seen amazing places.

We've struggled, too, like how to be married in 250 square feet, how to fix things on the RV, what to do when we had nowhere to stay, or outrunning a snowstorm by driving all night.

We've literally reinvented ourselves. We've created a better life not by having the perfect day every day, but by being present to what is happening and accepting it—finding the lesson or joy in it. Embracing it and soaking it all in. Like the water soaking into my socks on that dark Dallas night—I transformed cold, wet rain into pure warm joy.

Accept what is and let it in. That's how RVing transformed us. It can transform you, too, if you let it.

Camille Attell

If you want to learn more about Camille, how she makes money on the road and how she might be able to help you, check out her two websites listed above.

Camille and her husband, Bryce, travel in their large Class A motorhome.

Here's a totally different option—traveling in a van.

Another RVer Tells His Story

My friend, Scott Watson, travels in a small van with his cat, Luke. It's a fancy van, but it's still small. It's a fully decked out Winnebago Travato 59GL camper van.

He works full time for the same company he worked for before he hit the road, but now he does it from all over the country. He has four different Internet services to make sure he always has Internet access.

I asked Scott to tell us some of the good, bad, and ugly things he's experienced while living and working on the road. You might call this story a "slice of life." Here's his story.

Scott working in his camper van

The Rules Have Changed

The rules we grew up with about how the world works are rapidly changing. It's now possible to travel full time before retirement. Work can be more fulfilling than just paying the bills. And "success" is being defined less by how big a person's bank account is and more by how satisfied they are with their life.

Too many people settle for just surviving, but since you're reading this, you're probably not one of them.

It's time to define for yourself what success looks like. It's time to dust off those long set-aside dreams and truly live.

The RV lifestyle allows you to explore places and learn new things like no other way. Why? You slow way down to a much slower, manageable pace to learn what to do, see, and taste from locals. The brown roadside signs point you to interesting things that are normally passed up, but with an RV you quickly detour to explore that point of interest the brown sign points to. New discoveries are behind most brown informational signs.

For example, a brown sign alerted me to the Buffalo Bill Museum off the interstate highway, which caused me to deviate from my planned route. By deviating and stopping, I learned a tremendous amount at the museum, which includes a tour of an actual Mississippi riverboat. From that stop, I discovered a charming small town on the Iowa bank of the Mississippi River. I found a small-batch distillery in town that produced a fine selection of whiskey products.

As a bonus, the museum is a Harvest Hosts location, which means I get to stay in their parking lot overnight for free. I woke up to a glorious sunrise reflected off the Mississippi and got to watch early morning fishermen going out for the day's catch!

BAD - RV Parks

I have a love-hate relationship with RV parks. While providing a safe refuge from parking trouble, and a great place to empty waste tanks and fill with fresh water, they often provide little in the way of scenery. And strangely, they lack interactivity with short-duration RVers as most keep to themselves even though our "homes" are literally six feet apart.

UGLY - Internet Connectivity

We live in a connected world. Many, including full-time working and living RVers such as me, require Internet connectivity. While coffee houses, brewpubs, and RV parks say they have Wi-Fi, it's often so slow it's useless. So, I rely on cellular-based hot spots to provide the connectivity. While they function quite well, there are limits to the amount of data you can use before the carrier throttles down the speed to a near useless point. So, doing a lot of work on the internet, you will probably need to have more than one cellular data hot spot (expensive) or constantly be searching for productive Wi-Fi from a commercial establishment.

My best practice now is to use an app at "Speedtest.net" to speed test an establishment's Wi-Fi speed BEFORE I make any purchase (like coffee or food). If their network is too slow to be useful, I move on to the next business offering Wi-Fi. This process saves me money and time by not committing to a location until I know I can get the through-put needed to effectively do my job or upload YouTube videos

Crappy Internet speed and the search for good connectivity is the ugliest part of RV living that I have experienced. Oddly, this has nothing to do with the actual RV rig itself.

Scott Watson

You can follow Scott on his website at the link below. https://gosmalllivelarge.com/

And you can follow him on YouTube. Below is a link to his YouTube channel. https://www.youtube.com/channel/UCNiSQ74bY7cSn emOl5B-2yw

Bottom Line: I think you can see from the stories presented in this chapter that whether something is good or bad is mostly a matter of how you look at it. In other words, it's your attitude. After all, there are solutions to most RVing problems.

Chapter 3

You're Worrying about the Wrong Things

"There is nothing better than a friend, unless it's a friend with chocolate."

—Charles Dickens

Anyone who is thinking about living in an RV (whether it's full time or part time) will find a lot of things to worry about. Some of the things they worry about maybe need to be worried about.

At least they deserve some thought and attention. Maybe thought, concern, or attention are better words than worry anyway, but you get the point.

Many (maybe even most) of the things that people who are thinking about the RVing lifestyle worry about just flat out should not even be on your mind and for sure you don't need to worry about them.

Some things you shouldn't worry about

- **Security and safety** are the two things that a lot of people are concerned about when they think about hitting the road as a full-time RVer. When you're in a campground surrounded by other RVers, you are a lot safer than you are in your present stick-and-brick house or apartment.

  There's no riff-raff in an RV park and there is not much of anything of value that anyone could steal from an RV. If someone tried to break into your RV, one scream would bring help faster than calling the police. Lock your doors, take reasonable precautions and don't worry.

  If you're boondocking out in the middle of nowhere, the one precaution you should take if you have a camper is to invest in one of the secure locks for your hitch so no one can hook up to your camper and tow it off while you're gone.

In a nutshell, lock your doors, don't leave portable solar panels, generators, bicycles, or other expensive items outside while you're gone and take a reasonable amount of precaution.

Helen Keller said it best when she said,

"Security is mostly a superstition. It does not exist in nature, nor do the children of men as a whole experience it. Avoiding danger is no safer in the long run than outright exposure."

Most people tell me that the only time they have worried about being safe is before they hit the road. After they're on the road, they realize that they are not concerned about safety at all.

- **Loneliness.** A lot of people worry about being lonely. This is especially true for people planning on being a solo RVer. Don't worry about it. It will never happen. RVers are the friendliest people on the planet. You will have plenty of people to sit around the campfire with and enjoy casual conversations. You will also quickly develop deep friendships with a lot of RVers that you only see a few times a year but you stay in touch with. I have more friends now than I ever had before I started living the RVing lifestyle.

- **What if I decide I don't like the RVing lifestyle?** After you finish reading this book, I think you will know whether the RVing lifestyle is a life you will like or not. But as a backup plan, in case you don't like the lifestyle, as I describe in Chapter 13, RVing is a lifestyle that's easy to get into and easy to leave.

Some of the things you should be concerned about

Here are a few things you should be concerned about and you should make backup plans for when these things happen.

- **Money problems.** A lot of concerns can be covered in this category.

  Unexpected breakdown or maintenance problems.

  You find that you're spending more than you expected (and you will).

  You lose one or more of your sources of income.

  All of these situations can be handled by starting out with a cash reserve fund. Don't leave home without it. Don't spend all of your available cash buying your RV or on a down payment for your RV. I would suggest you have an emergency fund of $5,000 available as a minimum, and $10,000 would give you a lot more breathing room.

- **Emotional aspects.** Fear and loneliness are not the emotions you should be worried about, but you should be concerned and prepared for a lot of doubts, constantly dealing with unknowns, living in a small space with someone 24/7, and being away from family and friends.

Bottom Line: Almost everyone who considers living the RVing lifestyle has a lot of worries. That's normal. But, realistically, if you do your homework, there's not much to worry about.

Sure, a lot of things could go wrong (and probably will), but nothing is catastrophic. There are solutions to all RVing problems. You'll just have to adjust your attitude, deal with problems, and realize that problems and things going wrong is part of the RVing life.

Chapter 4

Why Do You Want to Live in an RV?

"It's the possibility of having a dream come true that makes life interesting."

—Paulo Coelho

If I knew none of my dreams would ever come true, I think life would be boring.

That's why so many people buy lottery tickets. They have a very slim chance, but at least by buying a lottery ticket they have a chance of a dream coming true.

If your dream is to live in an RV, you can make that dream come true, and you don't have to win the lottery to make it happen.

But before you get too far into deciding if you want to live full time in an RV, start by seriously asking yourself why you want to live in an RV in the first place.

Is this just another one of your wild ideas?

When I ask people who are thinking about living full time in an RV why they want to do it, I get answers such as:

- I want to travel and see the country.

- I want to experience the freedom of getting away from it all.

- I want to be able to spend more time with my family or spouse.

- I want to cut my living expenses.

- I want to get out of the rat race.

These are all valid reasons why someone would want to live full time in an RV, but a lot of people have some different reasons. They may give some of the reasons listed above when asked, but they have some other reasons. Some people have reasons they may not even be admitting to themselves.

A lot of people want to run away from their problems whether they admit this or not. I think many (if not most) wannabe RVers have the thought in the back of their minds that if they get in an RV and take off, they will leave most of their problems behind.

Living in an RV won't automatically solve your problems

Living full time in an RV might solve a few of your problems, but it could make some of your problems worse. If you're thinking that living in an RV will be less expensive than living in a stick-and-brick house or apartment, it can be, but also it can be a lot more expensive.

Likewise, if you want to live in an RV, spend more time with your spouse, and fix some problems with your relationship, that could happen, but also it could make the problems worse.

Living in an RV is a great way to solve a lot of problems, but it won't happen automatically. If you don't make some changes, things could get worse.

Living in an RV will change a lot of things in your life, relationships, and attitudes, and it's a good time to make changes that will solve some of your other problems, but it won't happen automatically. You have to consciously make the decision to make changes in your life.

Of course, after you make the decision to make these changes, you have to follow through and actually make the changes.

Living in an RV won't change who you are

If you like to eat in expensive restaurants, own new cars, and have the latest gadgets, moving into an RV won't change your wants. Without a conscious effort to make changes in your life, you'll probably still find yourself spending money on these things after you move into your RV.

Living in an RV could be more expensive and more stressful than the life you're living now.

A lot of my family and friends say they wish they could live full time in an RV, or they say they will be happy when they get old enough to retire so they can live and travel full time in an RV.

When I think of each one of my family and friends, I can't think of a single one of them who would be happy (at least not for long) living like I am.

After me being on the road full-time in my motorhome for seven years, not a single family member or friend has chosen this lifestyle. And it's a good thing they haven't because they would not be happy living like I live.

Living in an RV is not the right lifestyle for very many people

Even though it's a dream of a lot of people, the reality is that living in an RV is not the right life for very many people.

You will have to decide if it's the right lifestyle for you. I wouldn't want to live any other way, but it's probably not the right lifestyle for you.

On second thought, since you're reading this book, you're taking steps to do more than just dream about it, you're doing your research. So maybe it is right for you.

Just remember that living full time in an RV won't automatically solve all your problems and it won't get rid of all your baggage. You have to make other changes in yourself and in your life to make all that happen.

Everything you do when you're living in an RV will take some planning. Where do you dump your garbage? Where do the water and power come from? How do you get Wi-Fi? Where (and how) do you dump your black and gray tank?

Bottom Line: The full-time RV lifestyle is a *Happy Ever After* life only for the very few people whose personalities are compatible with it.

Give a lot of thought to why you really want to live in an RV. Then decide if your expectations are realistic.

Chapter 5

"I Wish I Had Waited Longer before I Started RVing," Said No One

"Travel is never a matter of money, but of courage."

—Paulo Coelho

Take another look at the quote above. It's so true, but most people don't want to admit it. Saying, "I can't afford to travel," is an easy way not to have to admit that they don't really have the courage to travel.

Getting back to the title of the chapter, I've heard a lot of RVers say that they wish they had started living the RVing life sooner, but I've never once heard anyone say they wish they had waited longer before they started or say that they started traveling too soon.

If you get into the RVing life and decide you don't like it, it's easy to get out of the lifestyle and go back to your previous life (or, even better, try another lifestyle).

And if you follow the advice in Chapter 13 about how to buy your first RV, and you buy a used RV at a price well below the market value, you can sell your RV and get your money back and maybe even make a small profit.

That way you can get into the RVing lifestyle, try it and then get out of it with no financial loss.

I devote a whole chapter to this topic. The title of Chapter 12 is *A Lifestyle That's Easy to Get into and Easy to Leave*, and it shows you exactly how to do it.

Finish reading this book and make sure you understand all the bad things that can happen when you're living in an RV (and believe me, bad things will happen), and if you still think you want to live full time in an RV, go for it.

The rules we grew up with about how the world works have all changed. You can now live full-time in an RV and not be retired. Chapter 11 goes over the many ways RVers are making money while living and traveling in their RV.

I'll give you a hint, it's now possible because of two things—the Internet and the change in the attitude of business owners and managers when it comes to hiring people to work outside the office.

It's now possible to travel full time before retirement, so there's no need to wait to start living the full-time RVing life. Well, maybe that's not completely true. There are a few reasons why maybe you can't start now. Here are some things to consider.

Some valid reasons why you might not be able to start RVing immediately

- You have two years left before you can retire and draw your pension.

- You won't start drawing your Social Security for another year.

- It's one more year before the kids are out of the house and off to college.

- You have one more year before your kid will be out of college.

- You have one more year before you'll finish paying off all your debt.

- You have one more year before your student loan is paid off.

- You have an aging parent you're taking care of.

- In six more months, you'll get your annual bonus.

These are some things to think about, and all not of these may be completely valid. You might be able to start RVing full time in spite of these obstacles. Get creative and see what options you can come up with.

This chapter is a little different from the others in that it may sound like it's trying to talk you into living full time in an RV rather than telling you bad things about the lifestyle.

Let me explain. The title of the book indicates that it's going to be talking about both the good and the bad parts of the RVing life, but you can't experience either one until you start living the lifestyle.

That's why I'm saying do your research, make your decision, and if the decision is to start living in an RV, make your plans and hit the road. You can always change your mind later.

A lot of people just never make a decision. And some people make a decision that's not based on a valid reason. It's a cop-out reason. It's like saying, "I can't afford it," when (like the quote at the top of the chapter says), they don't have the courage to do it.

What are the possible bad things about making the decision to live full time in an RV?

The really bad things you have to deal with when it comes to making a decision to live full time in an RV are not about safety. You'll be safer on the road than you are at home. Accept this fact. It's true.

Consider this quote.

"The fearful are caught as often as the bold."

—Helen Keller

If Helen Keller wasn't concerned about danger, what reason do we have to be fearful? She had a lot more unknowns in her life than we do for sure.

Franklin D. Roosevelt put it this way.

"The only thing we have to fear is . . . fear itself."

Below are a few of the fears you'll have to deal with

- Failure.

- Looking foolish?

- Having to admit that it was a bad idea if it doesn't work out.

- Looking like you didn't act logically or rationally if things don't work out.

All of these reasons come down to worrying about how you will look to your family and friends if things don't work out.

Even if everything works out great, some of them are still going to think you made the wrong decision, so don't worry about what people think. It's your life. Go live it.

Bottom Line: You've done all your research (if not, you can finish it in short order), and then you have to make a decision. If you think the RVing lifestyle is for you, go for it. If you're not sure, my guess is that it's probably not the right choice for you.

Here's another thing to consider. I hate to say it, but if you'll be traveling with a spouse and you're not both on board with the idea, it's probably not going to work out.

Chapter 6

Simplify and Go

"Our life is frittered away by details. Simplify, simplify."

—Henry David Thoreau

I don't know if ole Henry was talking about getting ready to live full time in an RV or not when he made the statement above, but it sure does hit the nail on the head. He died in 1862, so maybe not.

The best way to start living the RVing life is to just simplify and go. Work things out while you're on the road.

There are a lot of good, bad, and ugly things to think about when you're considering hitting the road as a full-time RVer.

What I see as the bad parts of getting ready to live as an RVer fall into two areas. People analyze everything to death, and they spend too much time trying to make a decision. Maybe these two things are actually just one thing.

What's worse than people taking too long to make a decision is some people never make a decision. Make a decision. You can always change your mind

You'll never have all the information

Every decision you make for the rest of your life will be made with incomplete information. Accept that fact, and your life will be a lot less stressful.

Do a reasonable amount of research, make your decision, and hit the road. You can make changes as you learn more and gain more experience.

When you hit the road, you'll learn more about RVing and learn more about yourself. Most people change how they like to RV after some time on the road. They may start out not wanting to boondock (camping with no hookups) and then end up boondocking a lot or vice versa.

Or they start out driving every day or every few days and then decide that they like to stay in one place longer or vice versa.

Buy a used RV and hit the road

A lot of people change RVs after a year or two on the road. Probably even more people would like to have a different kind of RV, but they're stuck with the one they have because they bought a new RV and owe more on it than it's worth.

In Chapter 13, I cover how to buy your first RV, and, in a nutshell, it says do NOT buy a new RV as your first RV. The key is to buy a used RV at a price that will allow you to resell it in a year or two and get your money back or maybe even make a profit on it.

Take my word for it. You'll want a different RV within two years. Surprisingly, most people want a smaller RV instead of a larger one.

The reason you can't do enough research to have all the answers is that one of the major variables is YOU. Books and videos can't explain how you will feel after you get started in the RVing life. You have to experience it. You might think you know how you will feel about the RVing life, but you'll find that you really don't.

You may find out that you don't even like the RVing lifestyle, but obviously you think you might like it or you wouldn't even be considering it.

RV living is not a vacation

The only way to know for sure whether living the RV lifestyle is something you want to do is to do your research and if you think you might like it, then hit the road and actually live the lifestyle for a while.

I don't mean try it for a week or even a month. You need to try it for at least a year to find out if it's right for you. I've heard people recommend that you rent an RV and go on a two-week RVing vacation. It might be fun, but it's a waste of money as far as gaining information about whether RVing is a lifestyle you'll enjoy.

There's no way you can know whether you'll like the lifestyle or not after only living it for two weeks. You won't know after two months either. The biggest mistake of this technique is that there's a big difference between a vacation and actually living the lifestyle.

Until you stop thinking of living in an RV as being on a vacation, you can't begin to know if it's the right lifestyle for you.

Even if you decide that it's not the right lifestyle for you (or for your spouse), there's a good possibility that going back to your previous lifestyle of living in a house, apartment, or condo is not what you want to do either. You're ready for a change.

If you think you might want to live full time in an RV, just do it. Buy a cheap, used RV. Take very few things with you (three shirts, your computer, a few tools, etc.). Well, maybe a few more things than that, but not much more. Decide what you need as you go along. I've never heard anyone say, "I didn't bring enough stuff."

What I mean by simplify and go

If you think you might like to live in an RV, don't analyze the idea to death. Just simplify and go. Most people way overanalyze the transition to living full time in an RV. They spend too much time making the decision and on top of that, they still make a lot of mistakes, do things wrong, and take too much stuff, and the biggest mistake of all is that they buy the wrong RV and spend way too much on their first RV.

If you think it's what you want to do, just simplify and go. Make changes as you go along.

By the way, take it slow when you start RVing. Don't travel all the time. Stay in one place for at least a few days (a week would be better). Everything you want to see will still be down the road next month and even next year.

Bottom Line: My friend, Lidia, travels as a solo RVer in her truck camper. Her motto is

"Listen to Your Soul. Simplify and Go."

I think those words sum up the whole decision-making process. Listen to your soul, inner voice, gut feel, heart, or whatever you want to call it, but after doing your research, you'll know if RVing is in your blood or not.

Just listen to your soul, make your decision and then the most important thing is to act on that decision.

You can follow Lidia's adventures on her YouTube channel at the link below.
https://www.youtube.com/channel/UCBq3rHmB_4Gp OCOPhgofzCQ

Chapter 7

What about Solo RVing?

"The man who goes alone can start today; but he who travels with another must wait till that other is ready."

—Henry David Thoreau

Ole Henry captured one of the best things about solo RVing in the quote above.

Not only can a solo RVer start and go when he wants to, but he can also go where he wants to go.

Are there more good or bad experiences associated with solo RVing? You can't find out by asking the people who are living as solo RVers because most people who are solo RVing like the lifestyle or they wouldn't be doing it.

For a lot of people when they think about solo RVing, the two things that come to mind are safety and loneliness.

Safety is not a problem at all. As I've said before, you are safer living alone in an RV than you are living alone in a house, condo, or apartment.

Will you be lonely?

As far as being lonely, that depends on the person. I have never felt lonely living in my RV, but I have friends who say they have felt lonely at times.

I've had RVing couples tell me that they get lonely at times. Even if they're surrounded by other people, it's people they don't know. For some people, it's easy to feel lonely when they're not around their family and friends.

My experience is that a lot of people think they might get lonely, but after they get on the road, they find that they're not lonely at all. In reality, they find that most RVers are friendly, and are happy to have somebody to talk to.

There's a lot of camaraderie when you're around a group of RVers.

Don't dismiss the fact that some people can get lonely when they're solo RVing. It's one of the possible bad things about solo RVing and if you're an introvert, it could be something you would have to learn to deal with.

It's all a matter of attitude

Whether solo RVing is good or bad is a matter of attitude. There are a lot of wonderful things about the lifestyle and there are plenty of things to get you bent out of shape and make you miserable.

I have been living as a solo RVer for seven years, and I wouldn't want to go back to living in a house or apartment.

I love the freedom of living by myself and I love living in an RV, but for sure, neither of these are right for everybody and probably not even right for most people. That's something you'll have to decide for yourself.

What are some of the good things about solo RVing?

There are a lot of good things about being by yourself whether you're RVing or not.

- You can go where you want to and when you want to.

- You can go to bed when you want to and get up when you want to.

- You can watch what you want to on TV.

- You can go out and be sociable when you want to be with people, and you can stay in your RV and be by yourself when you want to.

- You can fix what you want to eat.

- In a nutshell, solo RVing is about freedom.

What are some of the bad things about solo RVing?

Just like there are a lot of good things about solo RVing, there is also a long list of bad (or, at least, not so wonderful) things about it too. Consider the things on the list below.

- Being lonely and all the things that go with that.

- Not having anyone to help you do things.

- Not having anyone to help you make decisions.

- Even though, realistically, you are safe when you're living in an RV, you would still feel safer if someone was with you.

- When you're by yourself, you don't have anyone to help bring in some money to cover expenses.

- Not having anyone to share your experiences with.

- For some people, it could be depressing.

How do solo RVers describe their life?

If you go to YouTube and search for the phrase "Solo RVers" or "Solo Female RVers" or "Solo Van RVers" or any similar phrase, you will find dozens of videos. If you're thinking about RVing solo, I would recommend that you watch some of these videos. You'll learn a lot.

Keep in mind that most of the people in these videos are happy with their lifestyle. If they were unhappy or had experienced a lot of bad things, I don't think they would be creating and posting videos about their experiences.

Many of the videos do show real-life examples of the things that go wrong and the problems solo RVers have experienced. Whether you consider the problems they're dealing with as something bad or not depends on your attitude and how you look at the problem.

Of course, most of the videos make the solo RVing life sound wonderful, but if you read between the lines, you can see the problems and bad things they are dealing with. Then you can decide.

Since there are dozens of videos about solo RVing, which ones should you watch? Below are three that I would recommend (but keep in mind that most of these videos glorify the lifestyle and don't really point out the bad things).

Alex: YouTube.com/watch?v=3nMBNAlHQMo&t=5s

(Note: In the URL above the character between the "A" and the "H" is a lowercase "L" and not the number one.)

Becky: YouTube.com/watch?v=ebbo800_Rg0&t=2s

(Note: Becky had only been RVing for a little less than a year when this video was made, but now she has been living as a full-time RVer for almost eight years and still loves it.)

Pippi: YouTube.com/watch?v=X1EIdQN5rq0

(Note: In the URL above the character between the "X" and the "E" is the number one and not a lowercase "L."

By the way, contrary to a lot of other RVing videos, she does point out some of the bad things about living in an RV in this video.)

Almost everything that describes solo RVing could be considered a good thing or a bad thing. It depends on the person. The experience could be the happiest and most wonderful thing you've ever done or it could be the biggest mistake of your life.

I enjoy my alone time, but I have some non-RVing friends who start to go stir crazy if they're alone for very long.

Some things about solo RVing you can consider and decide whether you would like the lifestyle or not before you try it, but you may not be able to really know until you try it.

You may already be living alone in your apartment or condo, but it's not the same as solo RVing. You probably still have friends and neighbors nearby who are available when you want to socialize. When you're in a campground you're surrounded by people but you don't know any of them.

Some solo RVers have friends who travel with them for a week or more at a time. They say they're happy when someone is going to come travel with them for a week or two, but they find that they're also happy when it's back to just them being alone again.

Bottom Line: There are a lot of good and bad things about solo RVing. Most of it comes down to your attitude and personal preferences.

I don't know a single solo RVer who is not happier than they've ever been in their life, but if they weren't enjoying their lifestyle, they would be doing something else. In other words, take my observation with a grain of salt. It's not a scientific sampling of solo RVers for sure.

Chapter 8

What about a Home Base?

"Blessed are the cracked, for they shall let in the light."

—Groucho Marx

Everyone who takes the plunge to live in an RV has to decide what they're going to do about a home base.

There are two different home bases you have to be concerned about. The first one is a legal home base or legal address. Even though you may be traveling around and not staying in one place more than a night or two, you still have to have a legal address.

It's called your domicile. What address is on your driver's license? Where are you registered to vote? Where do you get your mail? Etc.

By the way, most people choose Florida or Texas. Another option, and the easiest thing to do (and a lot of people do it this way), is to keep your domicile in the state where you're living now. Set up a mailbox at a local UPS store and have a trusted friend or relative check your mail every now and then. That's what I did.

The second type of home base is not required, but a lot of RVers have one. It's where you go when you want to go home. A lot of RVers who are not full-time RVers keep the home they had before they started RVing. Others go back to their parents' houses, one of their children's houses, or visit a sibling or a friend. It's usually in the town where they used to live, where their friends are, and where their doctors are.

They usually still sleep in their RV, but it's a place where they store some things. It's also a place where they have access to tools and a place to work on their RV, and a place where they can leave their RV when they want to travel internationally, take a cruise, or whatever.

Of course, some people (like me) don't have a physical home base. I do have a mailbox in a UPS store and that is my official address. Except the NC highway department wouldn't accept that address to go on my driver's license, so I used my brother's address.

There is no one right answer. And even if you decide on the right answer for you, there's a good chance your answer will change in the future as your situation changes.

The most common RV lifestyle

A lot of people don't want to RV full time and they keep their home and live in it when they come back. Most of their stuff is still there. This is probably the most common way to RV. My guess is that there are more part-time RVers than there are full-time RVers.

When I'm talking to people in campgrounds and someone tells me that they're not living in their RV full time, they almost say it like they're apologizing. I think some people feel like they have let the RVing community down.

Remember, there is no right or wrong way to RV

Do it the way that makes you happy. Keep in mind that whatever you decide, there's a strong possibility that you will change your mind as time goes by. I've seen it go both ways. What's the perfect solution for you now could likely not be the perfect solution in a few years. I know a lot of people who sold their house and most of their stuff and started out RVing full time but then, after a few years of full-time RVing, they decided they wanted a home base. Sometimes it's back in the town where they used to live and sometimes it's in a completely different part of the country. Sometimes they buy a small condo in an area they've found that they like, and they live there part of the time.

Sometimes they buy a little piece of land in a part of the country they have found that they like. That way they will have a place to park their RV. They still live in their RV, they're just not on the road all the time. That's one of the many ways to RV.

What to do about having a home base

Not having a home base and having total freedom to travel anywhere you want to sounds like heaven. But for some people not having a home base can seem closer to hell than heaven.

Eric and Brittany solved their problem about what to do about a home base. They named their latest motorhome, basecamp. That way when they are out running around in their jeep, they can decide to go back to basecamp. Sounds like a good idea to me. You can find Eric and Brittany's blog at

http://rvwanderlust.com/

Jason and Candace named their Class A motorhome The Mothership. RVers do have a sense of humor and they tend to get creative when naming their RVs. You can find Jason and Candace on their YouTube channel at CampingWithTheKellys. Below is a link to their YouTube channel.

https://www.youtube.com/channel/UCsYG0BMZagWI o55up2XdZnw

Keep in mind that you are considering living the RVing lifestyle (whether it's full time or part time) because you want to experience a different way of living. You are not deciding how you want to live the rest of your life.

Bottom line: Just because you chose a way of life doesn't mean you are required to stick with it. You are free to change your mind anytime you want to. We RVers are known for having our plans carved in Jell-O. We are free to change our minds at any time and we often do. We don't have to apologize to anyone when we decide to change our minds and live a different way.

Chapter 9

Getting the Courage to Hit the Road

"Courage is knowing it might hurt and doing it anyway. Stupidity is the same thing. And that is why life is hard."

—Dr. Jeremy Goldberg

Whether your friends and family think you're doing the right thing or not by hitting the road and living in an RV probably has a lot to do with how much courage you will have to have when it comes to making the decision and taking the plunge into living full time in your RVing.

We would all like for our family and friends to agree with our decision and think we're making the right choice, but the truth is that they probably won't. I think Steve Jobs summed it up best when he said...

"Don't let the noise of others' opinions drown out your own inner voice. And most important, have the courage to follow your heart and intuition."

—Steve Jobs

Would Your Friends Like the RV Lifestyle?

The short answer is, "Probably not."

At least, most of them wouldn't like the lifestyle. If they wouldn't like it for themselves, it's hard to imagine how they could be happy about you living this lifestyle. Don't worry about what they think or about making them happy.

Sure, you would like it better if they would all think you were making the right decision and doing the right thing, but it's not going to happen.

It takes a special kind of self-reliant, independent, and adventurous person to be happy living in an RV.

Is RVing just a dream for you?

A lot of people dream of the freedom and adventure that come to mind when they think of living the RVing lifestyle, but that's all it is for them, just a dream. They don't have that burning desire to make RVing happen.

If your friends are like mine, a lot of them say, "Oh, I would love to live in an RV."

Then they follow that comment with a "but." The "but" statements go something like this:

- but I have too much stuff.

- but I couldn't be away from my grandkids.

- but I could never live in a space that small.

- but we could never afford it.

- but I would be too scared by myself.

- but I think I would be too lonely.

- but I'd be afraid I wouldn't like it.

- And the list of excuses (I mean reasons) goes on and on.

I don't try to convince people to live in an RV

The reason I don't try to convince people to live the RVing lifestyle is because I don't think most people would like it, even though they kind of think they would.

In all fairness, I think some of my previous ten books on living in an RV do sound like I'm trying to convince people to live the RVing lifestyle because I make it sound so enjoyable. Maybe I am. I think it's like somebody talking about their grandkids or their dog. It's hard not to talk about just the good things. That's why I wrote this book. I wanted to correct my ways and be realistic about the topic.

There are some people who will be living the RVing lifestyle in due time, but they can't do it right now. They have to wait another year or two before they can retire, or before they can start drawing their Social Security, or they have to sell a business, or sell their house, or wait until the kids finish college, or they're taking care of an aging parent.

Most of these reasons will disappear in time, and these people will hit the road and enjoy the RV lifestyle. You don't have to convince them. They've made up their minds, and they have a plan.

I don't want to try to convince anyone to abandon their present lifestyle and live in an RV until they're ready.

What you can learn from the movie, *City Slickers*

In the movie *City Slickers*, Curly said to Billy Crystal's character, Matt, "You spend fifty weeks a year getting knots in your rope and then you think two weeks up here will untie them for you." It doesn't work that way.

You already know that two weeks on a vacation won't fix all the problems in your life. When you start RVing, you'll realize that two months on the road in an RV won't solve all your problems either.

Curly also said to Billy Crystal, "The secret of life is one thing." When Billy asked him what that one thing was, Curly said, "That's for you to figure out."

Bottom line: Even though a lot of people dream of enjoying the freedom and adventure of the RVing lifestyle, most people will never take the leap and make it happen, and they probably wouldn't be happy if they did. The lifestyle is not for everybody—just you and me (and a few other adventure-loving souls).

Chapter 10

How Much Does the RVing Lifestyle Cost?

"It's nice to get out of the rat race, but you have to learn to get along with less cheese."

—Gene Perret

Asking how much it will cost to live full-time in an RV is like asking how much it costs to live in a stick-and-brick house. For a lot of people, the answer is simple, it will cost just a little more than you make.

That can be true for living in an RV or a house, but it doesn't have to be.

One of the biggest advantages of living in an RV is that you can cut your cost of living to almost nothing for a short amount of time, and then, when your sources of income improve or you save up the money to replenish your emergency fund, you can go back to living on a higher level of income.

Let me explain

If you're living in a conventional house, condo, or apartment, and you get laid off from your job, or have a large unexpected bill that uses up all your savings such as, you need a new roof on your house, or the transmission goes out in your car, or you have a major medical expense not covered by insurance, etc., there's not much you can do to immediately cut your living expenses.

You can do a few things to cut back on your expenses. You can stop going out to eat, you can stop buying things, and maybe you can put off making repairs to your house or car, but that's about it.

But if you live in an RV, you can temporarily cut your living expenses to the bone in a heartbeat. You can start boondocking and not pay any campground fees. You can stop traveling and not have any expense for gas or diesel fuel. You would still have basic expenses like insurance, food, cell phone service, etc., but that's about it.

Live this way for a short time until you have replaced your lost income or until you have replenished your emergency fund, and then go back to enjoying living in a higher income bracket.

If you live in a conventional house or apartment, there's not much you could do to cut your expenses. You could move into a cheaper apartment (after your lease expires), but there's not much you could do immediately.

By the way, as explained in the next chapter about making money while on the road, it is strongly recommended that you have multiple sources of income when you're RVing. That way it's unlikely you will lose all your sources of income at one time. You may lose a major source of income, but if you have several sources of income, you'll still have some income, so you won't use up your emergency fund as fast while you work on getting another source of income.

By all means, as pointed out before, don't start living full time in an RV until you have an emergency fund set aside. Remember that your emergency fund is for true emergencies and not for things you want to buy.

It's easy to live on way less than you make when you're living in an RV.

One of the big advantages of living in an RV is that your living expenses are not fixed.

I heard one friend say, "If traveling were free, you would never see me again." Well, it's not free, but it can be less expensive than living in a traditional house or apartment.

Of course, it could be a lot more expensive also. When you're RVing, you have a lot of control over how much it costs you to live. You don't have much control over your expenses when you're living in a stick-and-brick house.

A lot of RVers post articles and YouTube videos showing how much it costs them to live full time in their RVs. I've described some of these and linked to them below.

There's one thing to keep in mind about most examples of what it costs to live in an RV, and that is that most of them are talking about cash flow and not actual real costs.

For example, they don't include the depreciation on their RV, and it doesn't include the decreasing value of their tires. Tires are only good for five to eight years whether you drive on them or not. Most of the blogs and videos are just talking about the out-of-pocket expenses.

The next time you hear somebody say they are RVing on less than $1,000 a month, they may be, but make sure they are talking about their actual real costs and not just their cash flow or out-of-pocket expenses.

If you buy a used RV (maybe a very used one), and you do some work fixing it up, it may not decrease in value much at all, and if you bought it for less than it's worth (it's possible to do that if you do your homework), you may even be able to sell the RV for more than you paid for it.

I have a friend who does this once or twice a year. You have to know what you're doing and know the value of RVs. You can't recognize a bargain if you don't know what a certain make, model, and year RV is worth. As my father used to tell me, "You make your money when you buy something—not when you sell it."

Examples of RVers living on $1,000 a month or less

The idea of living in an RV for $1,000 a month or less might sound unbelievable, but seeing is believing, and below are links to a few short YouTube videos where RVers are showing how they're doing it.

If you go to YouTube and search for the phrase "RVing on $1,000 a month," you'll find dozens of videos of people telling you how they're doing it, and many of them show a detailed breakdown of every penny they spend.

Keep in mind that these are not typical or average RVers. These are some of the most frugal RVers. Obviously, it can be done. I just don't want you to think that this is typical or average.

The bad part is that you should realistically plan on spending more than $1,000 a month to live full time in an RV. If you notice, most of the people claiming to spend $1,000 or less a month do not include any amount for depreciation in the value of their RV or in the value of their tires. They are not including any amount for maintenance (unless they actually paid for some repairs that month).

Many of them are showing how much they paid for pet food, but they are not showing an amount going into an account for pet vet bills. It's not unusual for a pet to have vet bills of $1,000 to $2,000 or more from time to time. You have to budget for this if you have pets.

Here are links to the videos I promised you. (Note: YouTube adds about 3,000 new videos every day, so if you go to YouTube and do a search, I'm sure you can find dozens more videos on the topic and find more up-to-date videos.)

YouTube.com/watch?v=fvP2XHMDdE4&t=9s — In this video Kyle and Olivia talk about how much they spend living full time in their RV. They go a little over the $1,000 a month number and spend about $1,300 a month, but that includes making payments on some credit card debt and paying off a student loan. So, their actual cost to live in their RV is about $1,000 a month. (Update: In the spring of 2019, they had a beautiful baby girl, Nora, so now I'm sure their living expenses are a little more.)

YouTube.com/watch?v=XL60tPbY2YE — Here is a link to Robin's video where she discusses her budget and explains how she lives on a little less than $1,300 a month. She also shows you where she could get her living expenses down to less than $1,000 a month. For example, she spends $400 on food for one person. She could cut some out of that for sure. I assume that she is eating out a lot.

YouTube.com/watch?v=sKRY6dR7Ae4&t=202s — Eric shows how he lives full time in his Class C motorhome and spends $655 a month, and that includes $100 a month on his cat. He doesn't show anything in the budget for maintenance, but he can add $100 or so for maintenance and still be well under $1,000 a month.

YouTube.com/watch?v=VduibSuyHA4 — Bill goes over five years of his expenses and he spent a little over $1,000 a month, but as you can see he spent a lot of money on traveling and other things that you wouldn't spend if you were on a tight budget.

YouTube.com/watch?v=g_OmZzZD4rg — In this video, Sam breaks down his monthly costs and shows how he spends $1,650 a month, with $330 for gas and $450 for campground fees. He could travel less and boondock more and get his expenses below the $1,000 a month level.

YouTube.com/watch?v=VdZ0HWyoMjQ&t=11s — In this video Toby explains how he lives in a Ford Transit Connect van and spends $750 a month.

Becky Schade at InterstellarOrchard.com posted that she spent an average of $1,098 one year, $1,275 one year and $1,333 another year. She doesn't have a pet, but she does do a lot of driving.

Sue at RvSueAndCrew.net posted that her average expenses were $1,260 a month. She spends $130 a month on pet food. She does mostly boondocking and doesn't spend much (if anything) on campground fees.

Bottom Line: Don't let all the videos, blogs, and books (mine included) that talk about it being possible to live full time in an RV for $1,000 a month or less fool you into thinking it's easy to do.

Yes, it can be done, and a lot of people are doing it, but it's not easy. You have to learn to live in a very frugal manner. You can't go out to eat much, you can't buy a lot of new clothes or new gadgets like the latest cell phone or computer, and for sure you can't do many tourist things.

Chapter 11

Making Money While on the Road

"You have to be odd to be number one."

—Dr. Seuss

There are a lot of ways to make money while on the road. You could work part time in the gravel pit with Fred Flintstone, but there are easier ways to make money on the road.

You could have your own business, but don't kid yourself. You're not in business until you have a client or start making sales.

Maybe you can still work for your same employer

One of the first options you might want to consider is whether it's possible to continue to do your same job and work for your same employer but just do it remotely from the road and maybe do it part time.

At first, you might think that option wouldn't be possible in your situation, but don't dismiss the idea until you give it some thought and consideration. I know a lot of RVers who are doing just that, continuing to work for their previous employer.

Even though you think there's no way your present employer would ever agree to it, don't give up until you ask and present your case. First of all, finding good workers in today's job market is not easy, and finding someone with your skills and experience could be even harder.

Given the choice of having you work remotely or losing you altogether, it might make your employer seriously consider the idea of allowing you to work remotely.

When you're working remotely, there are a lot of advantages to your present employer. Be sure to point these out. Here are some benefits to your employer that you can point out.

- He won't have to provide an office for you.

- You could save him money by cutting your hours back and only working part time.

- You could even volunteer to work for less money. After all, you won't be spending time and money commuting to work.

- With Internet and cell phones, you can almost always be available.

- I'm sure you can think of other advantages in your particular situation.

Workamping

Workamping is a trademarked term owned by the subscription service, Workamper News. You can find them at www.Workamper.com.

As the name implies, the term describes working while you're camping.

There are a lot of ways RVers make this work. Most state and national parks (and a lot of private campgrounds) hire campers to do work at the campgrounds. They get free camping and, in some cases, they also receive payment in addition to the free camping.

They work at jobs such as working in the office, working in the gift shop, cleaning the bathrooms, checking campers in, etc. They generally put in about twenty hours a week.

Amazon hires thousands of RVers for the three months before Christmas to work in one of seven warehouses to pack and ship all the extra packages they ship during the Christmas season. They provide free camping and pay $15/hour with a lot of overtime.

It's hard work. You work a lot of hours, and you're on your feet all day, but you make good money. A lot of RVers work hard these three months and make almost enough money to live on for the rest of the year.

As long as you can pass a drug test and apply early, it's pretty easy to get hired.

Here's a link to Amazon's site describing the opportunity.

https://www.amazondelivers.jobs/about/camperforce/

Harvesting sugar beets in North Dakota is another popular workamping job. It's very hard work. You work fourteen days in a row working twelve hours a day. You get paid a little over $13.00 an hour and get time and a half for all the hours over eight hours a day. It's hard, dirty work, but if you can handle it, you can make good money.

Here's a link to more information about the job.

https://www.theunbeetableexperience.com/

Here's a link to a YouTube video where RVer Becky Schade, (someone who has been there and done that), describes her experience working harvesting sugar beets.

https://www.youtube.com/watch?v=WJif-6TihVI

Here's a link to Becky's blog where she describes more about beet harvesting.

https://interstellarorchard.com/2017/10/14/sugar-beet-harvest-job-descriptions-and-recap/

More ways to find workamping jobs

Below are links to three websites that provide information about workamping jobs.

- CoolWorks.com

- Workamper.com

- Work-for-RVers-and-Campers.com

How about writing a book?

Another way to make money while living in an RV is to write books.

My book sales pay for my RVing lifestyle, but don't depend on income from your book sales until you actually see the money. It will take a while to write your book, and it may or may not bring in a lot of money.

I've written twelve books (ten of them about RVing), and some bring in a lot of money and some very little.

To help you write your first book, take a look at this YouTube video.

https://www.youtube.com/watch?v=ZkoltFuljlE

She recommends doing some tasks different from the way I do them, but her techniques work, and you can follow her recommended techniques for your first book. You can find other videos on YouTube where people tell you how to write a book. Watch several of them and learn different techniques.

You can write and publish a book on Amazon for absolutely zero cost if you do everything yourself, but I don't do it that way. I go to www.Fiverr.com and hire somebody to design my book covers, I hire a professional to proofread my book, and I hire one person to format the printed version, and a different person to format the eBook version. You can get all of this done for about $300 or so.

You can spend a little more and get a more professional book cover designed. That's what I do now. I had the cover of this book designed by Elizabeth Mackey at

http://www.elizabethmackeygraphics.com/home.html

Writing books won't bring in money immediately, but when you do get your book published, it can bring in money for years to come.

What should you do after you write and publish your first book? It's simple, you should write another book. How-to books are easier and quicker to write, but novels will bring in a lot more money—maybe ten times more money.

If you want to write a novel, you'll need to know how to write dialog, how to develop a plot, and other skills that you won't need when writing a how-to book. There are YouTube videos that teach you how to do all these things.

You don't have to be an experienced writer. I'm an engineer and I never made a grade better than a "C" in a college English class in my life. When I got the first draft of this book back from proofreader, he had found over 1,200 errors. I had other people read the book and they found even more errors. You might still find some errors. I hope not, but it's possible.

RVing and making money on the road

If you're serious about making money on the road, you need to invest $3.99 and buy this eBook. A paperback version is also available.

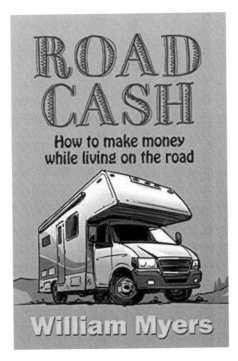

Here's a link to the book on Amazon. (Note: This is not an affiliate link.)

https://www.amazon.com/dp/B0721832MD

Below is a description of the book.

If you've dreamed of living on the road in an RV, camper or van, but wondered how you could afford to do it, this book is for you.

In *Road Cash*, you'll discover different ways to generate a decent income, how to make quick cash when you need it, and how to enjoy your life on the road while earning enough to pay your way.

I could write a chapter about all the different ways I've earned money while living full time on the road for seven years, but that wouldn't scratch the surface of the information included in this book.

Working for minimum wage when you're used to making five, ten, or twenty times that much may take some getting used to, but that's the price you pay for the freedom of living the RVing life.

One advantage of working these mundane jobs is that there are no corporate politics, you're not worried about getting the corner office, or a promotion, and you can quit anytime.

One last point

I highly recommend that you have more than one source of income. Having multiple sources of income means all your eggs are not in one basket. If you lose one source of income, you have other income to help cover your expenses while you replace your lost income.

Having multiple sources of income takes a lot of stress off you; plus, doing different things makes life more interesting.

Bottom line: It takes money to live full time on the road and in most cases, you won't be able to earn nearly as much money as you're making now. That's the bad part. The good part is that it doesn't take nearly as much money to live in an RV as it's costing you to live now.

I put more into savings every month now than I did when I lived in a stick-and-brick house and worked as an engineer. You can too.

Chapter 12

A Lifestyle That's Easy to Get into and Easy to Leave

"Be yourself; everyone else is already taken."

—Oscar Wilde

The RVing life may not be right for you. But if you've done a reasonable amount of research, watched YouTube videos, read some RVing books and followed some RVing blogs and you still think it might be what you're looking for, then by all means give it a try.

It might turn out to be the best decision you've ever made. I know it was my best decision ever.

But there are a lot of bad things about living the RVing lifestyle. And there are some really bad things. A lot of how you see RVing will depend on your attitude. Look at all the good and bad things pointed out in this book with an open mind and then decide if it's the lifestyle for you.

You can do research until you're blue in the face, but you still won't know for sure until you try it. At some point, you have to stop reading one more article or watching one more video and just decide.

Accept the fact that you don't know everything about the RV life. And if you keep doing research, you're just going to learn more about how wonderful it is. Books don't tell you many of the bad things about RVing (except this one). And when they do tell you something bad about RVing, it's usually in the form of a funny story.

RVing may not be right for you

If you're seriously considering the RVing lifestyle, accept the fact that it may not be right for you. But even if it turns out not to be a lifestyle you like, you probably won't want to go back to your existing lifestyle. You're ready to do something different.

You may decide you want to live on a boat, live in Florida, live on a farm, live in another country, or move to Timbuktu. (Yes, Timbuktu is a real place. It's a city in the West African country of Mali, and it's about as close to the middle of nowhere as you can get. It's not on my bucket list as a place I want to visit.)

Knowing that you're ready to do something different in your life, go ahead and get rid of your house and your stuff. You can always buy another house if you really want to go back and live in a subdivision somewhere.

I think you know that living the way you're living now is not making you happy. Go into the RVing life with the thought I'm going to give this a try, and if it's not what I want to do, I'll try something else.

If you really are not ready to part with your house (or your spouse is not ready), then rent it out for a year, but whatever you do, don't fret over the decision. Make the decision and move on.

Your house is a burden (even if it's paid for). Getting rid of your house is the first step to experiencing true freedom. When you get rid of your stuff and your house (by selling it or renting it out), you are free as a bird. You are free to live a totally different lifestyle. If you find that RVing is not right for you, you're free of your house and stuff and you can try another lifestyle.

Some decisions you make can be costly if it turns out to be the wrong decision, but that's not the case when it comes to deciding to live full time in an RV. That is if you do it the right way.

The right way to try the RVing lifestyle

Most of the truths you're learning in this book are about how a lot of things are not as good or wonderful as you've been led to believe, but this is one of the exceptions. The truth is that **you can buy an RV and later sell it and make a profit on the transaction.**

It's possible. I know plenty of people who have done it. The secret is that you have to buy your RV for less than it's worth. That can be done. The next chapter tells you how to do that.

You could say that you can try RVing with a money-back guarantee.

Bottom Line: The RVing lifestyle is easy to get into and easy to get out of because you can do it with no risk. Unlike other lifestyle choices you may want to try, RVing is one you can try with no risk. Just follow the advice in the next chapter about how to buy your first RV.

━━ Chapter 13 ━━

How to Buy Your First RV

"To travel is to live."

—Hans Christian Andersen

Most who are considering living the full-time RV lifestyle put way too much time and effort into deciding what kind of RV to buy.

I can understand. It's going to be their home. It's a big decision. There are so many options.

Do they want a Class A, Class C, a fifth wheel, or a camper? And then, after they decide what kind of RV, the question comes up about what size, and then whether to buy new or used, and if used, how used? There are almost an infinite number of questions that come to mind.

The truth of the matter is that it should be a simple process. There is only one criterion that has to be satisfied. You want to buy an RV that you can resell in a year or two and get most of your money back or even make a small profit.

Accept the fact that you will want a different RV within one to two years after you hit the road. There are two big reasons this is true.

The number one reason is that you don't know very much about RVs, so how could you possibly select the one that would be right for you?

The second reason is that there are so many different ways to live the RVing lifestyle, and different RVs work better for different RVing lifestyles. For example, are you going to be boondocking a lot or not at all? Are you going to be traveling a lot or very little?

Accept the fact that the way you want to RV will change

And even if you did know exactly how you were going to be living and the kind of RVing you would be doing, there's a good chance that the way you want to live the RVing lifestyle will change soon after you hit the road.

I have a friend who started RVing full-time and the one thing he was sure of was that he didn't want to do any boondocking. He wanted to stay in full-hookup campgrounds all the time. Within a year he decided that all he wanted to do was boondocking, and the RV he had was not very suited to boondocking.

It's fair to say that even if you did a lot of research and became very knowledgeable about RVs, you still wouldn't know how you will want to be RVing a year from now. It would be sheer luck if the first RV you picked turned out to be the right one for you. You're not that lucky, so don't even think it will happen.

Take a totally different approach

As I said before, your only criterion for selecting your first RV is to buy one that you can sell in a year or two and get your money back and maybe even make a profit (yes, it's possible).

Of course, this plan totally precludes buying a new RV. **Buying a new RV as your first RV is one of the worst decisions you could ever make.** You're almost sure to want something different within a year or so, and if you have bought a new RV, you won't be able to sell it without losing up to a third of what you paid for it—ouch.

One of the main draws of living the RV lifestyle is freedom and having options. If you buy a new RV, you no longer have as many options (at least not inexpensive options).

Yes, you can still decide where to go and how long to stay, etc., but you won't be as free to decide to get a smaller RV so you can boondock in more remote locations or get a more fuel-efficient RV so you can travel more without spending so much on gas or diesel fuel.

If you buy a used RV (and get it at a great price, meaning at below the market value), you have the freedom to change to any type of RV that fits your new wants and needs. You even have the option to completely leave the RVing life and not lose any money if that's what you decide to do. It's good to have options

Let's get on with how to buy your first RV

Okay, now you know your first RV should be a used RV that you can buy at a great price, and a great price means below the current market value. In other words, you want to buy it for less than it's worth.

Sometimes an RV dealer will spruce up a used RV and sell it for more than it's worth. And sometimes they just want to get rid of a used RV that they took in on trade when they sold a new RV and they will sell at a low price just to get rid of it.

You can't say that buying a used RV from an RV dealer is a bad idea or a good idea. You have to do your homework so you will know what's a good deal and what is not.

Likewise, a lot of RV owners who list their RVs on Craigslist don't realize how much RVs depreciate, and they think their RV is worth way more than it really is.

On the other hand, some people want to stop living the RVing life and just want to get rid of their RV. Maybe a spouse died or a couple decided they were too old to keep RVing. Whatever the reason, sometimes an individual seller is not necessarily looking to get the top dollar for his RV. They just want to get rid of it.

Keep in mind that just because a dealer or an individual is asking more for the RV he has for sale than it's worth, it doesn't mean you can't end up buying it for way less than his asking price.

Two things are necessary if you want to buy an RV for less than it's worth

The first thing is to know what the RV you're considering is worth. How can you buy it for less than it's worth if you don't know what it's worth?

Here are two easy ways to find out the true market value of any RV.

The first way is to check eBay and see what RVs like the one you're considering have actually sold for. Don't pay any attention to what someone is asking for an RV, and don't pay attention to the listed price of RVs that didn't sell. You only want to see what RVs like (or similar to) the one you're considering actually sold for.

To see the list of RVs that actually sold, click on the word "Advanced" in the top right corner of the page, and then, in the drop-down menu, put a check in the box for "Completed listings."

The second way to get a good idea of the price is to check out the website

pplmotorhomes.com/sold/soldmenu.htm

This company takes RVs on consignment and they sell about 2,000 RVs a year. You can find out what an RV of almost any type actually sold for recently by checking this site.

After you know what a fair market price would be for the RV you are considering buying, the next step is to negotiate to get a good price. (Remember, when you find the price that an RV like you're considering actually sold for, that's not the price you want to pay. You want to buy it for less than that price.)

Seven powerful negotiating phrases that get results

A lot of people don't like to negotiate, but when it comes to houses, cars, and RVs you have to. Sellers expect it and they don't quote you their best price to start with.

In most cases, the seller (dealer or individual) doesn't really expect you to pay their asking price.

Negotiating doesn't have to be a hassle or an unpleasant experience. Just use one or more of the seven statements below and watch the asking price start to come down in a hurry. If you use these statements, negotiating can be a fun experience.

#1. ALWAYS, ALWAYS flinch at the first price or proposal

You should almost fall over because you are so shocked. Do this even if the price you hear is way less than you expected. Flinch and say, "That's WAY beyond budget," and then shut up. Don't say a word. Just sit and wait for the price to drop.

#2. Next, when you get the lower price quote, you should say, "You've got to do better than that."

And again, you shut up. If you open your mouth, you won't get the next price concession. If you say yes to the first offer, the other person will know that they quoted you a price that was too low. They may even try to find a way to increase the price. They may say something like,

"Well, let me see if the boss will go along with this price," or, "Let me make sure that this is okay with my wife."

#3. If you make a counteroffer, ALWAYS ask for a much lower price than you expect to get

One of the cardinal rules of negotiating is that you should ask the other side for more than you expect to get. Henry Kissinger went so far as to say, "Effectiveness at the negotiating table depends upon overstating one's demands."

#4. Never offer to split the difference

It's human nature to want to "play fair;" our sense of fair play dictates to us that if both sides give equally, then that's fair. Realize that the other side is almost always willing to split the difference, so you should try to get a slightly better deal than that.

#5. How to use two powerful negotiating techniques all in one sentence. The two techniques are: "Absent higher authority" and "If I could, would you?"

We've all experienced the "absent higher authority" technique. For example, "Our insurance regulations won't let you go back in the shop," or "The loan committee wouldn't go along with those terms."

You don't get to talk to the loan committee (it doesn't exist) and you don't get to talk to the insurance company. It's a higher authority that you can't talk to.

Here's how to use the technique in your favor for once:

When you're down to the final negotiations, you can say, "If I could get my (financial adviser, spouse, or some other absent higher authority) to go along with this, would you replace the two front tires?"

Notice that in this statement you haven't agreed to anything.

The owner or salesperson is in a position of feeling that they need to go along with what you're proposing to keep the deal from falling apart.

#6. Nibble for more at the end

You can usually get a little bit more even after you have basically agreed on everything—if you will use a technique called nibbling.

You can say, "You ARE going to have the carpets professionally cleaned (or you ARE going to replace the windshield wiper blades), aren't you?"

#7. When you're getting close to the end of the negotiations and everything is just about nailed down, say, **"I'm getting nervous about this," and then SHUT UP.** The other party will think the deal is about to fall apart and they will likely throw in one more concession to seal the deal.

This technique works really well when a woman uses it. For some reason, men think women have a tendency to change their minds for no reason at all. (I don't know why men think that.)

One important point: If you're even remotely considering buying an RV, by all means, invest $3.99 and get a copy of Bill Myers' eBook, *How to Buy a Used Motorhome—How to get the most for your money and not get burned.*

This book is about buying a used motorhome, but a lot the information applies to buying a used camper/trailer. The book is also available as a printed book if you like printed books better than eBooks. Both books are available on Amazon at this link. The book has been recently updated, and this link takes you to the updated version.

https://www.amazon.com/dp/B007OV4TBY

Examples of what people bought for their first RV

Take a look at the RVs these people bought as their first RV and decide if you think they made good or bad decisions.

These are all examples of young people buying small RVs and it seems like they are all happy with their decision for now, but there's still a good possibility they will want something different down the road.

Here's a link to a YouTube video where Clarissa is showing us her RV that she bought for $5,000 CAD (about $3,700 US dollars). As of May 2019, she has lived in her van full time for two years.

https://www.youtube.com/watch?v=53_CwfdBBpg

Here is a link to a YouTube video where James and Rachel show how they live in their van. Watch the video and see if you can figure out why they named their van Sunshine.

https://www.youtube.com/watch?v=JszEEQg1cao

Elsa and Barron have lived full time for the past year in their 13-foot RV that they paid $3,700 for. Could you be happy in an RV this small? Don't answer until you watch their nine-minute video. Here is a link to the video.

https://www.youtube.com/watch?v=eA327Mtrex8

None of these examples describe the perfect type of RV to buy as your first RV. Maybe they're not even a recommended type of RV, but they do point out some of the many examples and options that are available.

I also think you'll agree that since these people bought their first RV at a great price, and then fixed and modified a few things, they could most likely sell their RV for more than they have invested in it. And that's your whole goal when you're buying your first RV.

Bottom line: This chapter is a little longer than most of the others, but as you can see, it's covering a somewhat complicated topic with a lot of options. Don't waste a lot of time trying to pick the perfect RV. Do a reasonable amount of soul searching and thinking about how you think you want to live the RVing life. Then find an RV (at below the market price) that looks like it will meet your needs. This gives you the freedom to get a different RV later when you know more about RVs and more about how you want to live the RVing life.

Chapter 14

What Are the Real Downsides to RV Living?

"It is good to have an end to journey toward; but it is the journey that matters, in the end."

—Ernest Hemingway

Since you're reading this book, my guess is that you've already been indoctrinated somewhat about how wonderful the RVing lifestyle is.

It is wonderful, at least a lot of people think it is, but that's not the whole story. Let me cover some of the not so fun and glamorous things about the RVing lifestyle that no one has told you about.

Here are some of the things that are not so wonderful about RVing

- If you like to work on things, there is always something on an RV that needs to be fixed. If you don't like to work on things, there is still always something on an RV that needs to be fixed.

- There's no way around it. You can't take all your "stuff" with you. You have to get rid of a LOT of things. For most people, getting rid of almost all of their stuff is the hardest part about getting ready to hit the road. The good news is that most people find out that they don't miss any of the stuff they got rid of and they are happier without it. (I know, you won't believe this until you actually do it.)

- Face it. There is not a lot of space in an RV. It's a totally different way to live. If there's going to be more than one person traveling, you could get on each other's nerves at times.

- RVs depreciate, and new ones depreciate fast. In a house, you're living in an asset that, hopefully, is going up in value. Just the opposite is true when you live in an RV. When most people talk about how much it costs them to live in their RVs, they leave out the part about how much their RV is decreasing in value each year. If you have an old RV and you're making improvements each year, maybe it's not depreciating much and maybe not at all, but the typical RV loses value every year.

- Medical care can be expensive if you're not old enough to be on Medicare. Not being close to your regular doctors can be a big problem if you have many health issues. Also, for most health insurance plans, when you're out of network, medical care gets a lot more expensive. This is discussed in more detail in Chapter 14. (Keep in mind that, as with all RVing problems, there are solutions to these problems.)

- For some people, constantly being away from friends and family (especially grandkids) can be a big problem. And for some people, it's a deal killer.

- For most people, when they become full-time RVers, they have to learn to get by with less income. If you like to go shopping, buy a lot of new clothes, and always have the latest gadgets, the RVing lifestyle might not be worth the sacrifices.

- Pipes in an RV are going to leak sometimes. It may be just a drip, or it could be a much bigger problem. The worst kind of leak is one you don't know about. You need to fix water leaks as soon as you find them. Even a drip can do major damage over time. Having a water pipe freeze and crack is one of the most common causes of leaks that you don't know about and then discover much later after the leak has done a lot of damage.

So, what's the real story when it comes to RVing?

If you want to know the pros and cons of living the full-time RV lifestyle, you might think that you could visit an RV park and ask several of the RVers there and get the real scoop.

But that's not the case. Most of the people you find in an RV park or in a boondocking place love the lifestyle. If they didn't, they wouldn't be there. You will get a one-sided view for sure.

If you watch many YouTube videos about the RVing lifestyle or follow any RVing blogs, you could end up thinking that RVing really is all rainbows, sunsets, campfires, and margaritas.

You can experience a lot of all four (with a little effort), but that's not the complete story.

It's kind of like Tom Sawyer describing how much fun it can be whitewashing a fence.

People who like the lifestyle can (and do) make it sound like heaven on Earth. People who hate it make it sound like being one step above (or maybe one step below) sleeping on the street.

The good parts of the RVing lifestyle

I could say it's all good. I don't remember any bad experiences. There have been times when things broke or stopped working, but that's just part of the adventure.

After all, if there were no unknowns or problems, there would be no adventure.

So, yes, there are many good parts of the RVing lifestyle. I'm sure you already have several ideas about why you want to live in an RV.

You can learn a lot more enjoyable things RVers like by watching some of the thousands of YouTube videos that other RVers have posted. Check out some of my favorite videos listed in Chapter 20, *Other Resources.*

Some of the things I like best about RVing include the freedom to go anywhere, anytime I want to. I love the people I meet, and I love the adventurous spirit they have. I like to see what's around the next curve or over the next hill. I know that sounds like a cliché, but it's how I feel. I truly love the RVing lifestyle. If I didn't, I wouldn't still be RVing going on eight years now—with no plans to change.

Continue reading this book and by the time you finish it, I think you will know enough to decide if RVing is the right lifestyle for you.

One thing to keep in mind is that one of the best things about choosing the RVing lifestyle is that if you decide it's not the right lifestyle for you, it's easy to sell your RV (and maybe even make a profit on it as I explained in the previous chapter), and then you can move on to a different lifestyle, such as living on a boat, living in a different country, living on a farm, living in two different places or whatever you think would be the best lifestyle for you.

How old is too old to RV?

Loren Phillips is eighty-seven and he just got back from a 13,000-mile trip to Alaska traveling solo in his Roadtrek RV. Below is an 11-minute video interview with him where he talks about his RVing experiences.

https://www.youtube.com/watch?v=tGIj8sDPfT0

When people ask me what I'm going to do when I get too old to drive my car, I tell them I'm going to put it behind my motorhome and tow it.

Bottom Line: It's true that the RVing lifestyle is not all rainbows, sunsets, campfires, and margaritas, but enough of it is that after living full time in my RV for over seven years, I wouldn't want to go back to living in a stick-and-brick house, condo, or apartment. No way. (And I don't even like margaritas.)

But one thing is for sure. The RV lifestyle is not for everyone, and in my opinion, it's not even right for most people. It takes a special kind of person to enjoy the RV life. Keep that in mind when you're watching videos and reading blogs and books that are telling you about how wonderful the lifestyle is.

Keep in mind that there really are a lot of bad and even some ugly things about the RVing lifestyle.

Chapter 15

The Good and Bad Things about Getting Rid of All Your Stuff

"A house is just a place to keep your stuff while you go out and get more stuff."

—George Carlin

I've heard a lot of people say, "I could never live in an RV. I have too much stuff."

I've never heard anyone say, "I choose to have all this stuff." They act like having a lot of stuff was something that happened to them (like being born with curly hair or being tall or short). They act like it just happened to them and there's nothing they can do about it.

The good things about getting rid of your stuff

When you have gotten rid of all the junk and stuff you don't need (which is almost everything you own), you will feel free and liberated in a way you can't explain or understand until you've done it.

Things will no longer control you. You will be in control of your life. You'll be free to do anything you want to do.

Also, it's a great feeling when you know everything you have and where it is. Never again will you have to say (or think), "I think I have one of those, but I'm not sure where it is."

If you need an item and you know you don't have it, that's good too. You won't waste time looking for the item. You can either decide to get by without it or you can go to Walmart and get it, or Amazon can have almost anything to you within two days.

The bad things about getting rid of your stuff

Most of the bad things about getting rid of all your stuff are not real. They are just in your head.

You'll think you'll miss things if you get rid of them. You won't. It's been seven years since I got rid of most of my stuff, and I have never missed a single thing.

I've never talked to another RVer who said they missed any of the things they discarded.

It's just the opposite. Every few months I go through my storage bins in the RV and throw away more stuff. Some of it is stuff I've accumulated in the last few months and some of it is stuff that I should have thrown away seven years ago.

Most of the things you'll want to keep and think you can't get rid of will fit into one of two categories. The item is either sentimental or you think you might need it someday. Neither one of those are valid reasons for keeping an item.

What about sentimental items?

Believe it or not, sentimental items are the easiest to deal with.

Pictures can be scanned and put on a thumb drive. That's even better than saving boxes of pictures. This way you can look at them easier and you can easily share them with friends and relatives.

Other sentimental items like, Grandma's lamp or the afghan Aunt Sarah made, can be given to other family members. This way they can enjoy them now, and if they won't take the item now, you know what will happen to the item when you're gone. They'll give it to Goodwill, or they'll throw it away.

I have a friend who started living full time in her RV. She had a ton of things she couldn't stand to part with, so she put them in a barn on her parents' farm. Two years later, the barn caught fire and everything in it was destroyed.

My friend said, "When I heard that all the things I cherished were gone, I was surprised that instead of feeling devastated, I felt a sense of relief. At first, I didn't understand the feeling.

"Then I realized that I had already taken the things I really wanted. The things I was storing were things that I didn't want. I just didn't want to get rid of them.

"Now all those things were gone, and I didn't have to feel bad about it because I didn't throw them away."

How to get rid of your stuff

This chapter is not about how to get rid of your stuff. It's about the good and bad parts of getting rid of your stuff.

I could write a whole book about how to get rid of your stuff. In fact, I did. The title of the book is Tidying Up. You can get the eBook version on Amazon at the link below for $3.99.

https://www.amazon.com/dp/0984496882

But unless you're having a really hard time getting rid of your junk, you won't need this book. Here's the condensed version.

Don't decide what to get rid of—decide what to keep

Everything sentimental should go. Everything else should go unless it really brings you joy. When you finish this process of getting rid of things, you'll still have way too much stuff, but at least you've made a good start. Nobody gets rid of enough stuff the first time around.

If you really can't get rid of all your junk, rent a storage unit and store things for a year, and then go through all the stuff again a year later and see what you think you need to keep (if anything).

I know one RVing couple who put things in a large storage unit and didn't even unlock it for seven years. They had paid a fortune for storing the junk for seven years. They finally went through the items again. They sold a few things, gave some things away, and put the rest in a dumpster.

Here's a phrase that might help you. *"If in doubt, toss it out."*

Here's another thing to keep in mind. Almost everybody wants a different RV after the first year or so, and surprisingly, most of them want a smaller RV. They want a smaller one because to start with most people go with a large RV (even though it seems small at the time) so they can carry all their stuff.

After a year or so, they realize they haven't used most of the junk they brought. It's just in the way. The smaller RV allows them to get into more camping areas. Most national parks were built back when RVs were much smaller, and sometimes larger RVs can't fit in the small campsites. Also, the larger RVs are harder to back and park.

The idea of getting rid of your junk (I mean valuable possessions) causes people more grief, agony, and stress than any other part of the process of moving into an RV. The sad truth (as most RVers will tell you) is that it should be a non-issue. In reality, it should be a fun and happy occasion.

Is your house just a high-priced storage shed?

That's the way a lot of RVers look at their house when they stop and realize how much stuff they have stored in their houses. The worst part is that almost none of it is being used. Their house really is just a storage shed.

One way to deal with the problem is to decide that you like your stuff more than you like the idea of living in an RV. Then do nothing and continue living like you're doing now. There's nothing wrong with this decision.

That's the decision most people make whether they say it or even realize it.

Of course, the other way to deal with it is to get rid of your stuff, buy an RV, and try that lifestyle for a while.

Bottom Line: There are good things and bad things about getting rid of your stuff. Most of the bad things are in your head. They're not real, but you have to deal with them anyway.

When (and if) you do get rid of your stuff, you'll experience freedom like you've never felt before.

Chapter 16

Is the Bad Part of RVing Really All that Bad?

"The only difference between a good day and a bad day is your attitude."

—Dennis S. Brown

The short answer: Yes, the bad part of RV living really is all that bad, and much worse than you've been led to believe.

Living the RVing lifestyle won't fix your relationship problems, it won't solve your financial problems, it won't make your wife and girlfriend get along, it won't get the IRS off your back, and it won't make your dog come as soon as you call him. In fact, it won't fix many (if any) of the problems in your life, and it for sure will add some problems to your world.

For example, after months of planning and taking care of every possible "what-if" situation they could think of, Nathan and Marissa broke down thirty minutes after they left on their full-time RVing adventure. They had to have their RV towed to a repair shop.

By the way, you can follow more of Nathan and Marissa's RVing adventures on their blog at

https://lessjunkmorejourney.com/blog/

You can also follow them on YouTube at

https://www.youtube.com/channel/UC2IENUorXc6kR tIiAGPRKZA

I'm sure breaking down thirty minutes after they started their RVing adventure was worse than anything they had expected or even imagined.

Whatever you can think of that might go wrong, sit around a campfire with other RVers for very long and you will hear someone talking about something worse than that happening to them.

There's no end to the things that can go wrong

I'm not talking about just mechanical breakdowns. There will also be times when you arrive at your reserved campground late at night to find out they have lost your reservation and don't have a place for you to camp.

Also, RVs will develop leaks. You just have to hope the leak is not directly over your bed.

Every time I think I've heard the worst story yet, I hear about something even worse.

The only thing you can do is to expect problems and go with the flow. The main difference between a bad day and an interesting day is your attitude.

If you can't handle things going wrong, then RVing is not for you. No amount of planning, preventive maintenance, or backup plans will prevent chaos from happening from time to time.

Buying a new RV for sure won't keep things from going wrong. It will be just the opposite. New RVs will have a ton of things wrong with them. One of the advantages of buying a new car is that you probably won't have any maintenance problems for a long time.

Just the opposite is true when you buy a new RV. You will have a lot of things that will have to be fixed in the first few months. These things will be covered by warranty, but it's still an ordeal to get them fixed.

How to deal with RVing problems

There are several things you can do to help you deal with the bad things that are going to happen when you're RVing. Here's what I recommend.

- Do preventative maintenance before you hit the road. Check fluid levels, tire pressure, and water levels in your radiator and batteries, spray everything that moves with silicone oil, etc.

- Carry a well-stocked toolbox with you.

- Have a Roadside Assistance policy. This policy will pay someone to come change a tire or tow you to the nearest RV repair shop. At least you won't be stranded beside the road.

- By all means, have an emergency fund. Having something break is bad enough, but having something break and not having the money to fix it is even worse.

- **The most important thing is your attitude.** Know that things are going to go wrong and things are going to break. Accept this as part of the RV lifestyle and go with the flow. How you deal with problems will have a lot to do with how much you (and the people traveling with you) enjoy the RVing experience.

Bottom Line: No amount of planning or backup plans will have you prepared for the things that are going to go wrong when you start RVing. I tell this to a lot of new RVers, but it doesn't sink in. They are still surprised when things really do go wrong.

Chapter 17

You Have to Hit the Road before You're Ready

"Don't wait. The time will never be just right."

—Napoleon Hill

If you're going to live full time in an RV, you have to hit the road before you're ready.

If you wait until you're ready, you'll never get on the road. You will never be completely ready. There will always be things you still need to do and questions that you still need answers to.

You will never have all the answers. I've been living full time in my motorhome for seven years, and there are still things on the RV that need to be fixed or modified. And I have a long list of questions I still don't have answers to.

For example, where is the fuse for the cigarette lighter socket? I use this for my GPS and to charge my cell phone. If I ever blow the fuse, I'm sure I can do enough checking and finally find the fuse, but it would be nice to know where it is now.

You have to make decisions with incomplete information. Realize that every decision you make for the rest of your life will be made with incomplete information. Make the decision and get going. You can always change things later when you get more information.

As Tom Watson, the founder of IBM, said, "Businesses have lost more money by not making a decision than they have by making the wrong decision."

He said basically to make a decision, and if it turns out to be wrong, you can always change things. If you don't make a decision and start, you can never get it right.

You have to set a departure date

To live full time in an RV you have to set a departure date. That's a date when you're going to hit the road come hell or high water. I can assure you that when that date comes, you won't be ready. There will still be things you need to do, and you'll still have a list of things to take care of.

Hit the road and work on the list of things you need to take care of while you're on the road. If you change your departure date once, you'll change it over and over.

The bad part of RVing that no one ever tells you is that there are 101 (or maybe 1,001) things that have to be taken care of before you hit the road. They won't all get done. They don't all have to be done. You have seen a lot of RVers on the road (and when you get on the road, you'll notice a lot more than you did before). One thing I can promise you is that not a single one of them had everything taken care of when they hit the road.

You're not like Lewis and Clark. You're not going out in the wilderness for two years with no way to communicate with anyone, or buy things you forgot.

You will still be able to fix things on your RV, get your mailbox service set up, change banks, close on the sale of your house, etc.

I know some people who say they are going to hit the road when they get everything taken care of and they have been saying that for years. I think the real problem is that they don't have the courage to take the leap.

Saying that they don't have everything taken care of is a face-saving way of saying that they don't have the courage to live full time in an RV.

Call a spade a spade (or maybe just call it a damn shovel), but whatever you do, don't hide behind the idea that you're not on the road yet because you don't have everything taken care of yet.

If you take the position that you're going to hit the road when you get everything done, it will never happen.

One of the good things about getting ready to hit the road as a full-time RVer is that when you set a date, mark it on your calendar, and tell all your friends the date you're leaving, it will take a load off you. It's a big relief knowing that it's really going to happen.

I have some friends who threw a going away party for themselves two months before their departure date and invited all their friends. That really made it official. They couldn't delay hitting the road after that. Don't delay your departure date even if it means that you pull out and then pull into a campground five miles from where you live.

Bottom Line: After you accept the fact that you're going to hit the road before you're completely ready, it takes a big load off your shoulders. Thinking everything has to be taken care of can drive you crazy. If you can't get your riding lawnmower sold, give it away to somebody who needs a lawnmower and can't afford one. You'll feel good about what you did, and you will have made somebody very happy.

Chapter 18

Why Haven't You Made a Decision?

"He that is good for making excuses is seldom good for anything else."

—Benjamin Franklin

Note: This chapter is not meant to convince you to live in an RV. In a way, it might sound like it, but the goal of this chapter is to convince you to make a decision. I don't want to talk you into or out of living the RV lifestyle. I just want you to decide whether you're going to do it or not. Here are some things to consider to help you make your decision.

Is hitting the road and living in an RV the right decision?

Is it what you want to do? You've gone over the numbers and all of the "what if" questions that keep popping into your mind a hundred times, but you haven't made your decision yet. Your gut feel or intuition is telling you that it's what you should do, but what is intuition anyway?

One dictionary definition of intuition is "the ability to understand something immediately, without the need for conscious reasoning."

We've all had many situations where something just didn't feel right about a place or a person and we've had times when we have said, "This just feels right. It feels like it's the right thing to do." We've all also heard the expression, "Trust your intuition."

But should you trust your intuition?

Instead of just a "yes" or "no" answer, RVers are inquisitive and also want to know "why" or "why not."

As an RVer, you constantly have to make decisions, like where to camp, whether to buy a different RV, if a venue is a good place to eat, and on and on. You make decisions all day long.

A lot of times you have a gut feel or intuition about a decision you are about to make, but should you trust that gut feeling? If trusting your intuition really worked, that would be a valuable tool or skill, or whatever you want to call it. But does it really work, and if so, why and how?

What is intuition?

Is intuition some super-power that some people have or is it like reading tarot cards or tea leaves?

The simple answer is no. Intuition is not some superpower, it's not magic, and it's not the universe looking out for us as one person told me.

You've probably heard of or experienced situations like the following two.

"Now that I'm pregnant, I see pregnant women everywhere." Or, "After I bought an Airstream, I see them on the road all the time."

In both cases, the pregnant women and the Airstreams were there before, but your conscious mind ignored them. But you better believe that your subconscious mind saw all these things and filed the information away in case it might be useful in the future.

There's a scientific explanation for how and why intuition works

Look at it this way. If you were the CEO of some big company (or even of a small company), you wouldn't want your employees bringing every little thing to your attention. You don't want somebody telling you that the commode is stopped up in the men's room or that the trash can is full in the break area. Your employees know not to bother you with this information.

But if your vice president had a heart attack, or your largest customer just canceled all of his orders, for sure you would want to know these things. Your employees know to bring these facts to your attention immediately.

That's the way your conscious and subconscious minds work. Your subconscious mind has a database of facts and observations that would make Google jealous.

Here's another example

Suppose you went to Walmart and had to park a long way from the front door. After walking all the way across the parking lot, when you got to the front door, if someone asked if you remembered the words on any bumper stickers you saw, there's a good chance that you wouldn't even remember seeing any bumper stickers.

If a video camera had been strapped to your head recording everything you looked at, and you went back and reviewed the video, you would likely see a dozen or more bumper stickers. You saw the bumper stickers, but that information was not recorded in your conscious mind because it was not considered to be important.

However, if you had a business selling bumper stickers or your job was to come up with phrases to put on bumper stickers, it's very likely that you would remember a lot about the bumper stickers you saw while walking across the parking lot because this information would have been brought to your conscious mind.

When you're RVing, pay attention and make good use of your gut feel and intuition. By all means, don't dismiss it as invalid information.

I don't know of any case where following my intuition ever caused me a problem, but I can think of some cases where I ignored intuition (or my gut feeling) and later regretted it.

Your subconscious mind is making use of hundreds or thousands of facts and observations to come up with a conclusion. This conclusion is sent to your conscious mind without ever revealing all of the data that was analyzed to reach that conclusion.

We are all procrastinators by nature and by habit. We've been making decisions and then putting off taking action all our lives.

Some people make things happen, some people watch things happen, and some people wonder what happened. To live the RVing life, you have to be a person who makes things happen.

Hopefully, you have already done the two hard things. You've made the decision, and you've set the departure date.

Now you have to **make things happen**.

You can't say, "I'm going to hit the road and live in an RV when I get everything taken care of or when (fill in the blank)." If that's your approach, it will never happen.

There are a lot of steps involved

To make your dream come true of living life as a full-time RVer, there are a lot of things that have to be done.

Everything has to fall (or be pushed) into place to make your RVing lifestyle a reality.

There are so many things you have to do or make decisions about that it's hard to even know where to start. It can seem overwhelming.

Of course, one of the first things you have to make a decision about (and then take action on) is what to do with your house.

If you're living in a rented apartment or condo, things are a lot simpler. The day your lease expires could be the day you hit the road.

But if you own a house, things get a lot more complicated. One of the first things you need to do is to take steps to get your house sold or rented. This will be one of your biggest obstacles. Take steps to solve this problem as soon as you make your decision to live in an RV.

Call a real estate agent and get your house on the market to sell or rent it. Tell your real estate agent that you want to set a price that will make your house sell in a reasonable amount of time. Then listen to what she tells you.

Don't sit around idle and wait for the house to sell. Since you've already set a date when you're going to hit the road, get busy taking care of the other things that must be done.

A word about selling your house. I know people who have had their houses on the market for two or three years and they still haven't sold them. A lot of people have an unrealistic expectation about what their houses are worth. Don't fall into this trap. It's worth what it will sell for now.

The main reason a house doesn't sell is that the owner has set an unrealistic price. Set your price at a fair market value (or maybe a little less) and your house will sell. Right now, houses are selling fast, so if you have set a fair price for your house, it will sell.

Put your house on the market, set a fair price, and if it doesn't sell within a reasonable amount of time, lower the price and keep doing this until it sells or until you decide to keep the house and rent it out. At that point, get it rented.

One other thing to be prepared for is that your house might sell within a few days. I was talking to a couple at an RV park recently and they said they had a contract on their house three days after they put it on the market. They had to get rid of everything and vacate the house in thirty days. My brother had a full-price contract on his house three hours after he put it on the market.

Another friend sold her house for the full asking price in about two weeks after it was listed. Houses are selling fast now and usually at or near the asking price.

Normally, getting a contract on your house is a good thing, but if you're not ready for it to sell, you might just have to get ready pretty quickly.

A few years ago, my neighbor had her place on the market for over a year and then finally sold it for less than she had turned down a month after it was listed. Your house is worth what it will sell for now.

My mother and father sold their house (and a lot of the stuff inside it) at an auction. Maybe you're not that brave, but a good auction company will get you a fair price for your house. I'm not recommending that you have an auction to sell your house, but if all else fails, it's an option.

If you don't have a deadline, you will never get to the end of your to-do list.

Start working on your list immediately

For example, you want to get your banking set up with two banks that have branches nationwide. It would be nice if this could be taken care of before you left, but you could do it while you're on the road.

You may want a better (or a lower-priced) car to tow behind your motorhome, or a different truck to tow your camper. You can sell your present car or truck and then buy something else while you're on the road.

Of course, if you're going to get a fifth wheel or a camper, one of the first things you will need to do (after you decide what kind and size of camper you want) is buy a truck.

You can't bring a camper home until you have a truck to pull it with.

Concentrate on taking care of the things that absolutely must be taken care of before you leave. Remember, you have a departure date. You'll be surprised how fast things happen when you really do have a firm departure date.

You always have the option of renting a storage unit for those items you're not ready to part with.

The next step is to start making things fall into place

After you set a date, take action. As I said before, the hardest thing for most people to do is to get rid of most of their "stuff," so start this process early—like now.

Adopt Larry the cable guy's motto of "*Get-er-Done.*" Another saying I like is, *"Done trumps everything."*

Not everything on your list will get done. In fact, not everything has to be done before you leave.

It's more important that you get things done than it is to get them done perfectly

You've been told all your life to do your best, but not everything needs your best effort.

For example, consider the situation where you're baking cupcakes and they crumble when you take them out of the pan. If you're baking them for the Cub Scouts, put more icing on the cupcakes and serve them.

On the other hand, if you're baking cupcakes for the bridge club, maybe you better start over and bake another batch.

My grandmother would roll over in her grave if she heard me say this, but...

If something only halfway needs doing, only halfway do it

That's the way it is with getting ready to live the RV lifestyle. Not every step in the process requires your best effort.

It's more important that you get rid of your stuff than it is to get the very best price possible for each item. Keep the big picture in mind and make sure you're making progress (and getting things done on schedule).

Once you've made the decision to quit your job and live in an RV, don't waste time second-guessing yourself.

Six months or a year down the road, you can reevaluate the situation and if living as a full-time RVer isn't making you happy, you can sell your RV, buy a boat, move to a different country or buy or rent a house or condo and live wherever you wish. You're not locked into your RVing decision permanently.

People ask me how long I am going to continue living full time in my motorhome. My answer is simple: "until it's no longer fun."

Back to reality

You made your decision before you got to this chapter. Don't keep rethinking your decision. This chapter gave you an overview of how to make it happen; now it's your job to follow through, implement the steps outlined and really make it happen. Get busy.

Bottom line: As you get closer to your departure date, it will start to feel like crunch time. There will be a ton of things that will still need to be done and not much time to do them.

You've handled crunch time and deadlines all your life, you can handle one more. This one is important. Make it happen. After all, you have a dream.

Chapter 19

Summing It All Up

"Normality is a paved road: It's comfortable to walk, but no flowers grow on it."

—Vincent Van Gogh

After reading this book, and learning about all of the things that can go wrong (and probably will go wrong sooner or later), if you still want to live full time in an RV, then I think you have what it takes to make this lifestyle work for you.

Realize that a lot of this lifestyle is not going to be fun, it's probably going to be more expensive than you expected, and your spouse (and probably even your dog) is not going to be happy with you all the time.

If you can accept all of this, and still want to live full time in an RV, then you can make it work, have fun and enjoy the adventure of your lifetime.

Living and traveling in an RV can be the happiest time of your life if you have (or can develop) the attitude of not letting things bother you and just go with the flow.

It's all a matter of attitude

I think you'll agree that a lot of videos, books, and blogs make the RV life sound wonderful. That's the problem. They all glamorize it.

Don't get me wrong. I love the lifestyle, but it can be a challenge. There are a lot of problems and a lot of bad things will happen. Whether you like the lifestyle or not will depend on your attitude.

Bottom Line: There are a lot of things you'll have to get used to. Sooner or later you'll have to deal with water leaks and things like sometimes you won't have much hot water. The list of inconveniences and problems goes on and on.

If you have questions for me, feel free to email me at

Jminchey@gmail.com

I would love to hear from you.

Chapter 20

Other Resources

"If you can't explain it to a six-year-old, you don't understand it yourself."

—Albert Einstein

This chapter contains information on resources that I think you will find helpful. Some of these links and resources have been pointed out previously in different parts of the book, but I'm including them here so you will have what I consider to be the most useful references all in one place.

I have placed the links in categories. Some of the links could fit into more than one category, but I tried to put them in the category they best fit in. You will find a few of the links listed in more than one category. I did this in order to make the categories more comprehensive.

Blogs that I follow

LessJunkMoreJourney.com – Nathan and Marissa publish one of my favorite blogs.

https://lessjunkmorejourney.com/blog

They also post a new YouTube video five days a week. Subscribe to their YouTube channel to be notified when new videos are posted.
https://www.youtube.com/watch?v=E6_AYrdfDS0

They are a young couple who sold everything and live full time in an RV with their toddler. Note: They recently added a baby boy to their family, and they sold their Airstream and bought a fifth wheel.

FollowYourDetour.com – Dan and Lindsay's blog is about creating your own path in life. It's about embracing change and taking risks in pursuit of a life you love.

Whether you've come to a dead end or are seeking an alternate route, following a detour is about the journey of self-discovery and growth. It's not about the destination. If where you're at isn't where you want to be, then it's time to follow your detour. Lindsay has also written a great book, *Follow Your Detour*. You can get it on Amazon at this link. The eBook version is only $3.99.

https://www.amazon.com/dp/B07PHJ5Y95

TheVirtualCampground.com/about – Liz Wilcox hosts a live one-hour YouTube video every Tuesday night from 7:00 p.m. to 8:00 p.m. where she interviews RVers from all around the country. You can find all the previous episodes and find out the topics of upcoming videos at the link below.

https://www.youtube.com/channel/UCTMhQeUuwXm CgOAcAW1zemA

You can find her book, *Tales from the Black Tank*, at this link.

https://TheVirtualCampground.com/book

As the title implies, it's a collection of humorous stories about RV life. One of my favorites is Alyssa Padgett talking about being locked in the shower in her RV for over an hour while her husband, Heath, was outside taking a walk. Get the book and you can see how it happened.

HeathAndAlyssa.com – Alyssa Padgett is a modern-day Renaissance woman. She runs a video production company, writes credible and consistent content for her website, and hosts the RV Entrepreneur Summit each February, all with her podcast-lovin' husband, Heath.

They do all this while living and traveling in their RV. If that wasn't enough to keep them busy, they just had a baby in the summer of 2019.

Alyssa has recently published a bestselling book, *A Beginners Guide to Living in an RV*. You can get it on Amazon at the link below.

https://www.amazon.com/dp/B0778WS6X4 ·

MoreThanAWheelin.com – Camille and her husband, Bryce walked away from their plush corporate jobs in 2016 to live full time in their new Class A motorhome. Since being on the road Bryce and Camille have started a blog called MoreThanAWheelin.com and launched Remote-Work-School.teachable.com to help people find remote work.

ChickerysTravels.com – Julie and Sean Chickery travel full-time in their RV and speak at RV shows all over the country. They provide a lot of information on their website. They have a new book out, *Full-time RV Finance – Second Edition,* that provides a ton of information and insight for anyone who is thinking about full-time RVing and wondering if they can afford it. You can find the book on Amazon at the link below.

https://www.amazon.com//dp/B07P5R48BY

TodayIsSomeday.net – Phil and Stacy Farley are both Navy veterans who decided to sell everything, grab life by the steering wheel and travel the country in an RV. They share their adventures on their website and on their YouTube channel, which is called *You Me, and the RV*. I follow every one of their videos. Here's a link to their YouTube channel.

https://www.youtube.com/channel/UCC3X81KrKId1Y vvl0Bs_VoA

RVOddCouple.com – *Here's their story.* We sold our house and most all possessions to hit the road and live in an RV full time with our toddler and dog. This is either the smartest or the worst decision we've ever made because we couldn't be more opposite. John is a night owl, libertarian, Irish, into '80s metal, impulsive, and loud. Mercedes is an early riser, liberal, Puerto Rican, into hip hop and Latin Pop, calm and reserved. They post videos every week and I watch them all. Below is a link to their YouTube channel.

https://www.youtube.com/channel/UC4xN2fR45tG0M 2Fm1w4PPTg

Technomadia.com – Cherie and Chris have been full-time RVing for over ten years. They say a technomad is a technology-enabled nomad. That's where the name of their website came from. They travel in a very fancy converted bus that they have geeked-out. Their site is a wealth of information for all aspects of RVing and especially for anything to do with technology or traveling.

They have written a great book, *The Mobile Internet Handbook*, which is the bible when it comes to getting connected to the Internet while on the road. They update the book often. You can find this book (and their other books and apps) on their website and on Amazon. (Note: They now live part of the year in their motorhome and part of the year on their boat.)

Wheelingit.us – Nina and Paul Wheeling travel in a Class A motorhome. Nina writes one of the most information-rich blogs on the internet. They do a lot of boondocking and she writes some wonderful blog posts on boondocking as well as traveling and other RVing subjects. Update: As of 2019, they have bought an RV in France and are still RVing, and Nina is still writing interesting blogs about traveling in their RV. But now the blogs are about RVing in Europe instead of in the US, and now they have a smaller motorhome.

GoneWithTheWynns.net – Nikki and Jason Wynn sold everything, bought an RV and off they went to discover the world—at least the part they could get to in their motorhome. They provide a lot of great articles and entertaining, high-quality videos that cover their travels, equipment, and all aspects of RVing.

Then, in 2017, they sold their motorhome and bought a catamaran sailboat and are living full time on their sailboat sailing around the world. They are adding a lot of articles and videos now about sailing, but the vast archives of RVing articles and videos on their website are well worth looking at. Reading their blog is fun, enjoyable, and informative. You'll love it.

InterstellarOrchard.com – Becky Schade is in her mid-thirties, college educated, and a single, female RVer who has been living full time in her 17-foot Casita camper for almost eight years now. She lives on a very tight budget and pays for her lifestyle by doing workamping at Amazon, working at national parks, and sometimes she does other gigs. She also supplements her income by writing. Her book, *Solo Full-time RVing on a Budget – Go Small, Go Now,* is a great book if you're on a tight budget and looking to get started RVing. You can find the book on her website and on Amazon. When you visit her website be sure to click on the link that says, "*Start here,*" in the top navigation, bar. It is useful stuff. She has another book out now, *The Little Guide to Dreaming BIG.* If you have a dream but it's not just the ordinary, everyday kind of dream, it's an unrealistic, crazy sort of dream that makes your heart sing and brings a little light into the dull routine of your day, this book is for you. (2019 Update: Becky has sold her small Casita and bought an even smaller tear-drop type camper.)

CheapRVLiving.com – Bob Wells has been living in a van for fifteen years. He boondocks most of the time and lives mainly off of his Social Security income plus income from writing, and occasionally he does some workamping jobs as a camp host. In addition to explaining how he lives, he also writes some great blog posts (which include wonderful pictures) about his travels and where he's camping. He also posts some interesting videos on his YouTube channel.

FloridaOutdoorsRV.com/page/top-rv-blogs – You can learn a lot from blogs and if you want to follow even more blogs than the ones I've listed here, this link will take you to a list of what are called the "**Top 50 RV Blogs**."

It also provides a brief description of each one. I don't follow all fifty of these blogs, if I did, I wouldn't have time to do anything else, but take a look at the list and see if any of them look interesting to you. My guess is you'll find some you like.

RV forums

Reading forums is a great way to learn about RVing. You can see what questions other RVers are asking (and see the answers being posted by fellow RVers). You can also get answers to your own questions. Here are the three popular RV forums I follow almost every day.

Rv.net/forum – Note that this website has a dot-**net** and not a dot-**com** suffix. The discussion group is broken into several categories—Class A, fifth wheels, Workamping, etc. Check out the different discussion groups and you will learn a lot. I check into these forums almost daily.

RV-dreams.ActiveBoard.com – This is an active discussion forum with the discussions sorted by topics. Check out the "Community Chat" section, the "Buying an RV," and the "RV Maintenance" sections or others that look interesting to you.

iRV2.com/forums – This is another active RVing forum that I check frequently.

Other RVing Forums – In addition to the popular forums listed above, there are forums for just about every brand and type of RV (Roadtrek, Airstream, National, Casita, Fleetwood, Forest River, Tiffin, etc.). Search Google and find the forum for your rig. It will be a great place to get answers to the many questions you will have about your RV. For example, "Where is the fuse for the cigarette lighter?" Your manual may not tell you, but someone on the forum for your type of RV will know and tell you almost immediately.

Finding campgrounds

Sometimes I pay full price for a campsite, but most of the time I get discounts of 50% or more. There are two main ways I get the 50% discounts. First, I can almost always get discounts of 50% or more by booking a campsite for a month at a time. That's what I usually do. The second way I get the 50% discounts is by using one of the websites or apps below:

PassportAmerica.com – Membership is $44 a year and you get a 50% discount at 1,900 campgrounds all around the country. Stay two or three nights and you've paid for your whole year's membership. I consider being a member of Passport America one of the best investments in the RV world.

AllStays.com – This site has a lot of campground and travel information. You can also get their information as an app for your iPhone, iPad, iPod or Android device at **AllStays.com/apps**

RVparking.com – This site has reviews and recommendations for 19,000 campgrounds. One thing I like about this site is that you get to see why people like or dislike a particular campground.

OvernightRVparking.com – Membership is $24.95 a year. They have the web's largest database of free RV parking locations in the US and Canada. Their database contains

14,237 RV Parking and No Parking locations in the USA and Canada. Search by your current location, city and state or province or zip code. Download PDF files by state or province.

UltimateCampgrounds.com – This site provides comprehensive information on over 31,000 public campgrounds of all types in the US and Canada. They also have an app.

America the Beautiful Senior Pass – If you're sixty-two or older and are a US citizen, you can purchase the *America the Beautiful National Parks and Federal Recreational Lands Pass.* It's also called the *Senior Pass.* It's $80 for a lifetime membership if you buy it in person or $90 if you want to receive it by mail. It allows you free admission and discount camping (which is usually a 50% discount).

If you're not sixty-two, you can get the Annual Pass with the same benefits.

You can get either one of the passes by mail by going to this website:

store.usgs.gov/pass/senior.html

To find locations where you can get the pass in person, go to:

store.usgs.gov/pass/PassIssuanceList.pdf

I recently camped at Curtis Creek campground in the Pisgah National Forest in North Carolina. There were fourteen campsites there and only two of them were occupied. With the pass, the cost was only $2.50 a night to camp and enjoy some of the most beautiful views in the North Carolina Mountains. You have to go about three miles up the mountain on a gravel road, but there is no problem getting a Class A motorhome to the campground.

FreeCampsites.net – This is a free website that allows you to search for free camping places. You can enter a city and state or a zip code and see a map showing free camping places. In most cases, there is information about each site in addition to its location.

HarvestHosts.com – This is a great resource for finding farms and wineries all over the country where you can camp overnight for free. Staying overnight at a winery or farm is a fun experience. Membership is $79 a year. They have 853 farms and wineries that are members and I find it well worth the membership fee. Harvest Hosts provides you the opportunity to travel to new areas, have unique experiences and enjoy purchasing locally grown and produced products. (Camping is free, but you are expected to buy a bottle or two of wine or some fruits or vegetables.)

CasinoCamper.net – Most casinos will allow you to camp overnight and many of them will even give you some free chips (they want to get you inside so you will start gambling). If your luck is like mine, this option might end up costing you more than just paying to camp at an RV park.

Walmart.com – Most people don't think of Walmart as an RV park, but most Walmart stores allow RVers free overnight parking. Last week, I spent the night in a Walmart parking lot and there were about forty other RVs there. They started coming in about 5:00 p.m. and most of them were gone by 8:00 the next morning. Be sure to call or check with the manager to get permission. In some locations, city or county ordinances make it illegal to park overnight in the Walmart parking lots.

BoondockersWelcome.com – This website lists hundreds of places where you can boondock free of charge. You will generally be camping in other RVers' driveways. It's $30 a year if you will only be a guest and $15 if you have a place and agree to also let RVers camp free in your driveway.

When you agree to be a host and let people boondock in your driveway, they don't just show up. They contact you and get permission. You only let people boondock at your place when it's convenient for you. If you're going to be out of town or having company, you probably don't want boondockers during that time.

I haven't used this website yet, but everyone I've talked to who has used it said they had a wonderful experience when they did. The hosts are friendly, gracious and happy to have you. They like to have fellow RVers to talk to and visit with.

CampgroundMembershipOutlet.com – At this site you can buy or sell a campground membership. You can get a great deal on a previously owned Thousand Trails, Coast to Coast or other campground memberships. If you travel a lot, you can save a ton of money with a campground membership. They are expensive to buy new, but you can get some real deals buying used.

RVing videos that I like

Search YouTube for the word "RV" and you will find five million videos. Some are extremely useful and informative; some contain bad and untrue information. Some are interesting and entertaining, and some are just plain boring.

I haven't watched all five million videos, but I have watched a lot of them (and I do mean a lot). Below are some of the ones I consider to be worth your time to watch. Turn off the TV and spend an hour or so watching these videos and you will be entertained and informed.

Many of the videos I have linked to here have been linked to previously in other chapters. I'm providing the links here so you will have all of the RV videos in one place.

Note #1. I have watched a lot of YouTube videos and one thing I've found is that on most videos I can speed them up to 1.5 speed and still understand what's being said. This allows me to watch more videos in the time I've set aside to watch YouTube videos. To do this click on the little gear symbol in the bottom right corner of the video and then click on "Speed." A pop-up menu will appear. Click on 1.5 and see how you like it.

Note #2. When you're watching these videos, you will see other videos on the page by the same people or about the same topic. Check out some of these. Watching YouTube videos about RVing is an entertaining way to quickly learn a lot about RVs and the RVing lifestyle.

Now I'll get on with the list of videos:

- **Vimeo.com/71385845** – I love this seven-minute video. It's about a young couple and their full-time RVing adventure traveling with a small child. Take a look at it. I think you'll like it too.

- **Youtube.com/watch?v=NGxmSGf2Kr8** – This fourteen-minute video shows 17 full-time RVers as they describe how they make a living while living the RVing lifestyle. If you're looking to make some extra money while you enjoy RVing, maybe you can get some ideas from these RVers.

- **Youtube.com/watch?v=g0UJAMNXJbk** – This eight-minute video is an interview with a retired couple describing their life on the road and how and why they decided to make the transition to the full time RVing lifestyle.

- **Youtube.com/watch?v=jAhBnq2pLNk** – This is another 8-minute video interview with a retired couple.

- **Youtube.com/watch?v=ebbo800_Rg0** – This eleven-minute video interview is with a young, single, female RVer. If you're thinking about being a solo RVer, I think you will find her story interesting. By the way, she has now been on the road for seven years and still loves the lifestyle.

- **Youtube.com/watch?v=E6_AYrdfDS0** – Nathan and Marissa have had four RVs in three years and in this video, they talk about what they wish they had known before they started their RVing life. (Note: Since this video was posted, they have changed from a Class A motorhome to an Airstream travel trailer, and then to a fifth wheel.) And by the way, they now have new member of their family. In the summer of 2019, they had a baby boy. He loves being a full-time RVer.

- **Youtube.com/results?search_query=rvgeeks** – This is a link to a list of how-to RV videos by RV Geeks. You will find a lot of useful information in these videos.

- **Youtube.com/watch?v=7AR4uOmGfxc** – This is a link to one of Kyle and Olivia's *Drivin' and Vivin'* Q&A videos. They are a young couple living full time in their tiny camper. Check out several of their videos. I think you will find them interesting. They are now in the process of renovating an Airstream camper. (Update: in 2019 they finished renovating their larger Airstream and they had a baby girl, Nora. Nora is a full-time RVer now.)

- **Youtube.com/watch?v=BsEs-CLBbaU&t=98s** – Marc and Tricia travel with their three kids and a Golden Retriever. They have posted several fun, interesting, and informative RVing videos.

- **Youtube.com/watch?v=c2xkfkhfcEg** – Nate and Christian Axness are a young couple who travel with their two kids. I think you will find their videos interesting.

- **TechNomadia.com/ramblings** – If you like the interview style of videos, this link will take you to dozens of these videos produced by Chris and Cherie at **Technomadia.com**

- **Youtube.com/watch?v=BfCuqhMe2r4** – This video shows you the simple way to back a motorhome into a campsite. Watch this video and follow the technique shown and you will be able to back your rig like an expert.

- **Youtube.com/watch?v=bkiK5ZUgLT8** – Here is a short forty-second video by Pippi Peterson. She is a young, single, female who lives and travels full time in her 1992 Class A motorhome. She posts a new video every week about her RV life on the road and, believe it or not, about RV maintenance and modifications that she does herself. She has now sold her Class A motorhome and is RVing in a fifth wheel.

- **Youtube.com/watch?v=xsiLyjgQyzE&t=118s** – In 2012 Lidia bought a 28-foot Class C motorhome and hit the road with her ten-year-old son. She later changed to a 28-foot travel trailer and then a truck camper. This video explains why she likes the truck camper the best.

- **Youtube.com/watch?v=xoy3vNUjLOU&list=PLezWHE RL6sh-HzlwkJb85waSxQ_VRPxkx** – Carolyn is a fifty-year-old, single woman who quit her high-paying corporate job and now lives full time in her 29-foot

Class C motorhome. In this video, she explains why she decided to change her lifestyle. (By the way, that's a really long link, but it is correct.)

RVing books that I like

With most eBooks priced at $2.99 to $3.99, you can get a lot of RVing information for very little money. Here are some of my favorite RVing books.

(Note: Many of these books have been linked to in previous chapters.)

Buying a Used Motorhome – How to get the most for your money and not get burned, by Bill Myers.

Don't even think about buying a motorhome without reading this book. The information in this book saved me thousands of dollars. And, even more importantly, it helped me pick the right motorhome for my needs and budget.

The book is about buying a used motorhome, but a lot of the information would also be useful and helpful if you were considering buying a travel trailer or fifth-wheel camper. You can find the book on Amazon at this link:

Amazon.com/dp/B007OV4TBY

Solo Full-time RVing on a Budget – Go Small, Go Now, *by* Becky Schade. You can find the book on Amazon at this link:

Amazon.com/dp/B00W30OFCE

Or you can find it on her website at **InterstellarOrchard.com**

She has another book, *The Little Guide to Dreaming BIG.* You can find it at this link:

Amazon.com/dp/B01HREJMZK

Road Cash – This book shows you step by step dozens of ways RVers are making money while living on the road. I read it and it's an excellent book. I have already been using some of the techniques talked about, and they work just as described. There are many other location-independent income-producing methods described that I'm eager to implement. Here's a link to the book on Amazon:

Amazon.com/dp/B0721832MD

The Mobile Internet Handbook - For US Based RVers, Cruisers & Nomads (2018 version) – This comprehensive guide to mobile Internet options for US-based RVers was written by full-time RVing technomads Chris and Cherie. You can get the book on Amazon at this link:

Amazon.com/dp/B079JW8W69

Convert Your Minivan into a Mini RV Camper by William H. Myers. For $200 to $300 and a minivan, you can have an RV that you can comfortably live in. You can find the book on Amazon at this link:

Amazon.com/dp/1530265126

How to Live in a Car, Van, or RV: And Get Out of Debt, Travel, and Find True Freedom by Bob Wells. You can find the book on Amazon at this link:

Amazon.com/dp/1479215899

RV Basic Training Manual – Motorhome Driving Course. Learn what every commercial driver MUST know, and every RV driver SHOULD know. The book is a little pricey at $30, but well worth it. It's a forty-six-page manual with a lot of pictures and drawings, so it's easy to read. You can order it at this website:

RvBasicTraining.com/buy-manual.html

Get What's Yours – The Secrets to Maxing Out Your Social Security by Laurence J. Kotlikoff and Philip Moeller. The book has been revised to cover the new laws. You can get the book from Amazon at:

Amazon.com/dp/B00LD1OPP6

The book you're reading is the tenth book I've written about the different aspects of RVing. You can find a complete list of my RVing books in the right panel of

my website at **LifeRV.com** or look at the last two pages
of this book for a list. They are all available on Amazon.

RVing novels

If you're looking for some great novels with plots built
around RVing, I would recommend the Mango Bob series.
The series includes *Mango Bob, Mango Lucky, Mango
Bay, Mango Glades, Mango Key, Mango Blues, Mango
Digger,* and his latest book, *Mango Motel.*

They all revolve around a thirty-five-year-old single guy
and his adventures as he lives and travels around Florida
in his motorhome. I have read all of the books in this
series and I love them. I think my favorites are the last
two, *Mango Digger, and Mango Motel.* I liked *Mango
Glades* too. It's hard to pick a favorite. I liked them all. I
listed them in the order they were published, but you
don't have to read them in any order. Each book stands
alone.

You can find them on Amazon at this link:

Amazon.com/dp/1889562033

RVing groups

Escapees.com – I recommend joining this group. It's
$39.95 a year and you also get membership in the new
Xscapers.com group (which is for younger RVers) at no

extra charge. With your membership, you will receive their printed magazine every other month. I consider this the most useful RVing magazine in the industry. They also offer discounts on insurance, camping, and a lot of other things I spend money on. Take a look at their website and see if you think what they offer would be useful to you.

RVillage.com – This is a free website and it's a great way to keep up with where your RVing friends are and let them know where you are.

FMCA.com – The Family Motor Coach Association is a popular group with RVers. The organization has been around for a long time. Take a look at their website and the benefits they offer. The cost is $85 for the first year and $75 for renewals. One of the things they offer is a program for getting great discounts on Michelin tires. They also host awesome RVing rallies. There were over 3,000 RVs at one of their recent rallies.

Getting healthcare on the road is changing

Important note: How the government will be changing healthcare options is totally unknown right now. I'm sure there will changes for 2020, so be sure to check the six websites listed below to get the latest information.

Here are six websites that will give you the latest information about getting healthcare when you're a full-time RVer.

- **RverInsurance.com**

- **RverHIExchange.com**

- **HealthSherpa.com**

- **Teladoc.com** – 24/7 access to a doctor, by phone

- **24-7HealthInsurance.com**

- **Kff.org/interactive/subsidy-calculator** – This is a link to a website that has a handy tool to provide estimates of health insurance premiums and subsidies for people purchasing insurance on their own in health insurance exchanges created by the ACA (Affordable Care Act). It will most likely be updated to include information on new programs that become available. Check it out.

How to find work as an RVer

If you're RVing full time or thinking about it and want to do some part-time work while you're RVing, the websites below will be useful to you.

CoolWorks.com – This is a free site.

CoolWorks.com/jobs-with-rv-spaces – This link goes directly to a page on the above website that probably has what you're looking for.

Workamper.com – This is a subscription website. The cost is $39.95 a year.

Work-for-Rvers-and-Campers.com

Apps

AllStays.com/apps/camprv.htm – This is the app I use the most. With this app, I can find reviews of almost 30,000 campgrounds, find locations of dump stations, find overhead clearances, and even find grades on steep mountain roads. It costs $32.95 to download the app to your iPhone or Android device.

RVParking.com – This app contains almost a quarter of a million reviews of 20,000 campgrounds. The price is right for this app—it's free.

US Public Lands: You can find information about public lands with this app:

TwoStepsBeyond.com/apps/USPublicLands

About 34% of the land in the US is owned by the government. Almost all of it is out west. If you've ever wanted to know where to camp free on government land, you'll love this app. This app shows BLM, Forest Service,

NPS, and public land boundary maps. You can download the app from Google Play or iTunes.

Reserve.WanderingLabs.com – When you check for availability at a campground and there's no campsite available on the dates you want to camp, instead of checking back every few days, let this app do it for you. Instead of checking back every few days it will check every few minutes and send you an email as soon as a space becomes available.

The app is free, but if you want to make a small donation, you can get the version that checks constantly instead of every few minutes.

Waze.com – Your smartphone can be a reasonable substitute for an RVer-specific GPS. By RVer-specific GPS, I mean one that gives you information about bridge clearances, grades, dump stations, etc.

Having a hands-free phone holder in the RV is key for this.

This app also has real-time info on road conditions, traffic backups, and speed traps. It's called Waze. You can download it at **Waze.com**. I really like it. The price is right too—it's free.

Other websites

Spend an evening or two reading the articles and watching the videos you'll find on the websites listed below and you'll know more about RVing than most of the RVers out there. Best of all, I think you'll find the way the information is presented in these videos, blogs, and articles to be enjoyable and entertaining.

I check these websites for new information at least once a week. Most of them have a way to sign up and get an email message alerting you to when new information is posted.

Technomadia.com – Chris and Cherie hit the road in 2006 and haven't looked back. They share a lot of useful information on their site. They have a big converted bus that they have done wonders with and made it fancy and functional. Spend some time on their website and you will soon know a lot more than most long-time RVers. New articles are posted every week and there are a lot of video interviews on this site that you will find interesting. Note: They spend half of their time now living and traveling on their boat.

RV-dreams.com – Howard and Linda have a website that's full of information and personal experiences. Turn the TV off and spend a night reading and absorbing the wealth of information they have to offer. There is also a lively discussion forum on the site. You can find a link to their discussion forum in the left Nav. panel on their site. Howard was an attorney in his previous life, but he gave that up to live full time in an RV.

InterstellarOrchard.com – Becky Schade is in her mid-thirties, college educated, single female living full time in her RV. She does workamping and writing to fund her travels. On her site, you can read her articles and you can learn more about what she does and her solo RVing lifestyle. She posts a couple of new articles every week and I think you will find them enlightening and interesting. Some of her articles are about her travels and some are about what she does, what she thinks and her life in general on the road as a full-time single female RVer.

CheapRvLiving.com – Bob Wells has a ton of information on his website about living in a van. He has lived in it full time and traveled for many years. He lives mostly on his Social Security. Check out his website and see how he does it.

Motorhome.com/download-dinghy-guides – Some cars can be towed with all four wheels down and some require that you use a dolly. At this site they offer downloadable guides. They have a different guide for each model year. If you already own a car that you're considering towing, be sure to check your car's owner's manual to see if it can be towed with all four wheels down.

Pplmotorhomes.com/sold-rvs – This site tells you what RVs have recently sold for. The people at PPL Motorhomes sell about 2,000 motorhomes a year and they show you what each one actually sold for. They also always have a huge inventory of used RVs for sale. Most of them are on consignment.

RVSchool.com – This is a great RV driving school. They teach you to drive in your own motorhome. Take a look at their schedule and see if they're going to be offering training at a rally near you. They offer discounts at most RV rallies.

Use **Yelp.com** to find recommended local services—dentists, restaurants, auto repair shops, computer repair shops, etc.

There are thousands of good sources of information on the internet (and, of course, thousands of sites with information that's not so useful). The links I have provided in this chapter are to the RVing resources (books, forums, videos, apps, and websites) that I use the most and the ones I think provide really useful and trusted information. I highly recommend you take a look at all of the resources I have linked to in this chapter and throughout the book.

If you have questions for me, feel free to email me at **Jminchey@gmail.com** or go to my website at **LifeRV.com** to learn more about the RV lifestyle and adventure. On the website, you can post your questions in the discussion forum and you will get answers from me and other RVers.

Whether you enjoy the RVing adventure or whether you find it frustrating will be determined a lot by your attitude. Spend some time watching the videos and reading the blogs that I've linked to in this chapter and I think when you realize how much fun other RVers are having and how much they are enjoying the adventure, it will help you realize how wonderful this lifestyle can be.

Note that after you read this book, and watch a lot of the YouTube videos I link to, you may decide that the RVing life is not for you. The purpose of this book is to give you the information to make an informed decision.

RV products I love – You may have noticed that I don't promote or endorse many RVing products in this book or on my website. None of the links I provide are affiliate links, and I'm not compensated for any comments I make about any product. I endorse only the few products that I truly believe in. Here is one such product:

BattleBornBatteries.com – If you're considering upgrading your RV battery bank, you can't go wrong going with the Battle Born lithium-ion battery to replace your present lead acid battery bank. Battle Born lithium-ion batteries seem expensive at first, but when you consider they come with a ten-year warranty, and that you can get almost twice the useful amp-hours out of them because you can almost fully discharge them instead of only discharging them down halfway like you do with a lead-acid battery, you will begin to see the advantages of converting your RV to a Battle Born lithium-ion battery. In the long run, they are the lowest cost RV battery option.

And if you hang out with the CEO of Battle Born, Denis Phares, very long, you'll learn that he is a great guitar player.

Bottom Line: If you're considering becoming an RVer, realize that there is a lot to learn in order to safely and economically enjoy the RV lifestyle. Check out the links in this chapter (and the rest of the book) and you will be well on your way to being an informed and experienced RVer.

Keep in mind that there really are a lot of good things, a lot of bad things, and a few downright ugly things about the RV lifestyle.

Did You Like This Book?

If you liked this book, I need your help.

I would really appreciate it if you would take a minute and leave a review on Amazon. (You can do it in only one minute.)

Writing a review is not like writing a high school book report. All you need to do is write a sentence or two saying that you liked the book.

Thank you,

Jerry Minchey

On the following pages are some of my other RVing books that you might find interesting and entertaining.

(You can find them on Amazon.)

Other books by the author available on Amazon

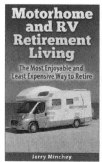 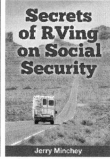

More books by the author available on Amazon

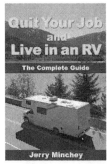 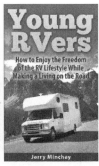 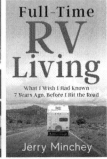

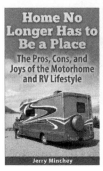 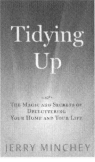 

Made in the USA
Las Vegas, NV
29 May 2022

49516534R00107